T0209717

An Analysis of

Keith Thomas's

Religion and
the Decline of Magic

Simon Young
with
Helen Killick

ROUTLEDGE

Published by Macat International Ltd
24:13 Coda Centre, 189 Munster Road, London SW6 6AW.

Distributed exclusively by Routledge
2 Park Square, Milton Park, Abingdon, Oxon OX14 4RN
711 Third Avenue, New York, NY 10017, USA

Routledge is an imprint of the Taylor & Francis Group, an informa business

www.macat.com
info@macat.com

Cataloguing in Publication Data
A catalogue record for this book is available from the British Library.
Library of Congress Cataloguing-in-Publication Data is available upon request.
Cover illustration: Etienne Gilfillan

ISBN 978-1-912302-77-2 (hardback)
ISBN 978-1-912127-15-3 (paperback)
ISBN 978-1-912281-65-7 (e-book)

Notice
The information in this book is designed to orientate readers of the work under analysis,
to elucidate and contextualise its key ideas and themes, and to aid in the development
of critical thinking skills. It is not meant to be used, nor should it be used, as a
substitute for original thinking or in place of original writing or research. References and
notes are provided for informational purposes and their presence does not constitute
endorsement of the information or opinions therein. This book is presented solely for
educational purposes. It is sold on the understanding that the publisher is not engaged
to provide any scholarly advice. The publisher has made every effort to ensure that
this book is accurate and up-to-date, but makes no warranties or representations with
regard to the completeness or reliability of the information it contains. The information
and the opinions provided herein are not guaranteed or warranted to produce particular
results and may not be suitable for students of every ability. The publisher shall not be
liable for any loss, damage or disruption arising from any errors or omissions, or from
the use of this book, including, but not limited to, special, incidental, consequential or
other damages caused, or alleged to have been caused, directly or indirectly, by the
information contained within.

CONTENTS

THE MACAT LIBRARY

The Macat Library is a series of unique academic explorations of seminal works in the humanities and social sciences – books and papers that have had a significant and widely recognised impact on their disciplines. It has been created to serve as much more than just a summary of what lies between the covers of a great book. It illuminates and explores the influences on, ideas of, and impact of that book. Our goal is to offer a learning resource that encourages critical thinking and fosters a better, deeper understanding of important ideas.

Each publication is divided into three Sections: Influences, Ideas, and Impact. Each Section has four Modules. These explore every important facet of the work, and the responses to it.

This Section-Module structure makes a Macat Library book easy to use, but it has another important feature. Because each Macat book is written to the same format, it is possible (and encouraged!) to cross-reference multiple Macat books along the same lines of inquiry or research. This allows the reader to open up interesting interdisciplinary pathways.

To further aid your reading, lists of glossary terms and people mentioned are included at the end of this book (these are indicated by an asterisk [*] throughout) – as well as a list of works cited.

Macat has worked with the University of Cambridge to identify the elements of critical thinking and understand the ways in which six different skills combine to enable effective thinking.
Three allow us to fully understand a problem; three more give us the tools to solve it. Together, these six skills make up the **PACIER** model of critical thinking. They are:

ANALYSIS – understanding how an argument is built
EVALUATION – exploring the strengths and weaknesses of an argument
INTERPRETATION – understanding issues of meaning

CREATIVE THINKING – coming up with new ideas and fresh connections
PROBLEM-SOLVING – producing strong solutions
REASONING – creating strong arguments

To find out more, visit **WWW.MACAT.COM.**

CRITICAL THINKING AND
RELIGION AND THE DECLINE OF MAGIC

Primary critical thinking skill: PROBLEM-SOLVING
Secondary critical thinking skill: EVALUATION

Keith Thomas's classic study of all forms of popular belief has been influential for so long now that it is difficult to remember how revolutionary it seemed when it first appeared.

By publishing *Religion and the Decline of Magic*, Thomas became the first serious scholar to attempt to synthesize the full range of popular thought about the occult and the supernatural, studying its influence across Europe over several centuries. At root, his book can be seen as a superb exercise in problem-solving: one that actually established "magic" as a historical problem worthy of investigation. Thomas asked productive questions, not least challenging the prevailing assumption that folk belief was unworthy of serious scholarly attention, and his work usefully reframed the existing debate in much broader terms, allowing for more extensive exploration of correlations, not only between different sorts of popular belief, but also between popular belief and state religion. It was this that allowed Thomas to reach his famous conclusion that the advent of Protestantism – which drove out much of the "superstition" that characterised the Catholicism of the period – created a vacuum filled by other forms of belief; for example, Catholic priests had once blessed their crops, but Protestants refused to do so. That left farmers looking for other ways of ensuring a good harvest. It was this, Thomas argues, that explains the survival of what we now think of as "magic" at a time such beliefs might have been expected to decline – at least until science arose to offer alternative paradigms.

ABOUT THE AUTHOR OF THE ORIGINAL WORK

Born in 1933, **Keith Thomas** is regarded as one of the greatest historians of post-war Britain, a reputation largely founded on his landmark text *Religion and the Decline of Magic*. Thomas invigorated historical research by turning to methods drawn from anthropology and sociology, intrigued by the potential of social history as a means of revealing the mind and thinking of early modern Europe. A humanist and a fellow of the British Academy and the Royal Historical Society, Thomas was knighted by Queen Elizabeth II in 1988.

ABOUT THE AUTHORS OF THE ANALYSIS

Dr Simon Young holds a PhD in history from Cambridge and now teaches at the Italica Academy in Florence. His research focuses chiefly on the traditions of English and Irish popular literature.

Dr Helen Killick holds a doctorate in history from the University of York. She is currently a Leverhulm Early Career Fellow at the University of Reading, where her work focuses on medieval economic history.

ABOUT MACAT

GREAT WORKS FOR CRITICAL THINKING

Macat is focused on making the ideas of the world's great thinkers accessible and comprehensible to everybody, everywhere, in ways that promote the development of enhanced critical thinking skills.

It works with leading academics from the world's top universities to produce new analyses that focus on the ideas and the impact of the most influential works ever written across a wide variety of academic disciplines. Each of the works that sit at the heart of its growing library is an enduring example of great thinking. But by setting them in context – and looking at the influences that shaped their authors, as well as the responses they provoked – Macat encourages readers to look at these classics and game-changers with fresh eyes. Readers learn to think, engage and challenge their ideas, rather than simply accepting them.

'Macat offers an amazing first-of-its-kind tool for interdisciplinary learning and research. Its focus on works that transformed their disciplines and its rigorous approach, drawing on the world's leading experts and educational institutions, opens up a world-class education to anyone.'

Andreas Schleicher
Director for Education and Skills, Organisation for Economic
Co-operation and Development

'Macat is taking on some of the major challenges in university education … They have drawn together a strong team of active academics who are producing teaching materials that are novel in the breadth of their approach.'

Prof Lord Broers,
former Vice-Chancellor of the University of Cambridge

'The Macat vision is exceptionally exciting. It focuses upon new modes of learning which analyse and explain seminal texts which have profoundly influenced world thinking and so social and economic development. It promotes the kind of critical thinking which is essential for any society and economy.
This is the learning of the future.'

Rt Hon Charles Clarke, former UK Secretary of State for Education

'The Macat analyses provide immediate access to the critical conversation surrounding the books that have shaped their respective discipline, which will make them an invaluable resource to all of those, students and teachers, working in the field.'

Professor William Tronzo, University of California at San Diego

WAYS IN TO THE TEXT

KEY POINTS

- Keith Thomas is a Welsh historian who was born in 1933. He was a pioneer in the study of the history of early modern* England.

- *Religion and the Decline of Magic* describes how and why beliefs about magic* changed in England between the years 1500 and 1700.

- The book broke new ground by demonstrating the value of considering history from the perspective of modern societies.

Who Is Keith Thomas?

Keith Thomas was born in 1933. A gifted student, he left his Welsh grammar school for Oxford University in 1952 and remained there for the rest of a distinguished career in several colleges. He retired in 2000.[1]

Thomas was one of a number of influential historians at Oxford in the period immediately following World War II.* Of these, the most celebrated was perhaps the Marxist* historian Christopher Hill,* who mentored Thomas both as an undergraduate and a graduate. Hill was the founder of *Past and Present*,* a historical journal that Thomas was later to edit.

Although Thomas concentrated on social history*—the study of the past from the perspective of the everyday people who lived it—he rejected the more uncompromising political model favored by Hill, and went no further than a flirtation with Marxism early in his career.[2] The intellectual climate of 1960s Oxford encouraged novel approaches to the study of history, however, and at this time Thomas opened himself to the influence of social anthropology*—a branch of the study of human cultures that emphasizes social and economic relations. He became interested in the work of prominent Oxford anthropologists who were active in that field, particularly E. E. Evans-Pritchard.* All of these influences can be seen in *Religion and the Decline of Magic*.

Published in 1971, this was Thomas's first book. Although he went on to write a number of other influential works, it remains the one for which he is best known. It has continued to be an important influence on historians, even if its conclusions and methodology have been challenged and many social anthropologists have found its anthropological models outdated.

What Does *Religion* Say?

Keith Thomas had in mind a single core question when he wrote *Religion and the Decline of Magic*: what caused the decline in the belief in magic in England between about 1500 and 1700?

To put it in more concrete terms: Thomas wanted to know why it was that an Englishman or woman in 1500 would have been more willing to explain their lives in terms of witchcraft*, ghosts, and spells than their descendants, living in 1700.

In the course of those two hundred years we see a shift in mentality intimately connected with the end of the "irrational" Middle Ages* and the rise of the "rational" modern world. Thomas's question, then, is fundamental to the understanding of the evolution of Western societies, and a satisfactory answer as to why this change took place would allow a historian to lay claim to one of the keys to modernity.

In *Religion*, Thomas uses methods drawn from the field of social anthropology to explore the thinking that led medieval people to believe in magic. His argument is that magic had a pragmatic function, and that it was designed to remedy problems, such as disease, for which there were no immediate solutions. In this way, Thomas illustrates how magic fulfilled a similar role to popular religious belief. He then goes on to examine how changes in orthodox religious belief and practice, and advances in science, together undermined magical belief and practice.

The work has had an immense influence on historians of all periods for a number of reasons.

First, the book represented a new way of looking at social history, uncovering previously unstudied aspects of the religious and popular life of early modern England. Second, by using social anthropology and comparative examples from the developing world, it also gave historians new methods of historical analysis. The primary impact of the book can therefore be viewed as *methodological* rather than *historical*; it mapped out new areas for research in the fields of both social history and intellectual history*—the study of the history of thought and thinkers—and presented historians with a new analytical approach.

Despite *Religion*'s ambitious scope, however, it is arguable that Thomas failed to fully answer the key question he had set himself.

Religion achieved the status of a classic in a matter of months after its publication in 1971. By 1973 one review was referring to it as "a magisterial and ground-breaking book."[3] The fact that it has been published in more than one edition, and in numerous reprints, and that it appears frequently on university reading lists, shows that it is still relevant today. *Religion and the Decline of Magic* also has a life outside academic debate because it is read both by historians and members of the general public. It was, for example, named in 1995 by the *Times Literary Supplement* as one of the one hundred most important postwar books "in public discourse."[4]

Religion was later published by the popular Penguin and Peregrine imprints and, in 2012, the Folio Society invested in an illustrated edition for the general reader, with an introduction by the famous British historical novelist Hilary Mantel.* The text also appeals to niche audiences like occult enthusiasts and those interested in folklore.[5]

Why Does *Religion* Matter?

At the broadest level, *Religion and the Decline of Magic* demonstrates the potential for social history to help us understand the belief systems and world-views of the past. Thomas makes the early modern period— that is, about 1500 to 1700—accessible by explaining its concepts in modern terms. This is particularly important in relation to magical thinking, something generally alien to modern thought. For example, he frequently points to the ways in which acts that seem at first glance to be irrational, and perhaps even silly, can help society to function. He explains the apparent success of "magical" practices by drawing on modern ideas such as the "placebo"* and "suggestibility," which highlight the roles our subconscious behavior and assumptions play in our health and actions.[6]

Another way in which the text can inspire today's students is as a model of the interdisciplinary method—that is, a method of research that draws on different fields of study.

Thomas turns to the disciplines of sociology and social anthropology, believing that these fields of study can bring general theoretical insights from other cultures. He draws on E. E. Evans-Pritchard's studies on African witchcraft, for example, to help us understand early modern English witchcraft.[7]

The idea that an anthropologist's work on a contemporary society could be useful to our studies of the past was exciting to an entire generation of historians. Even if the approach is less fashionable today than it was in the 1970s and the 1980s, the idea that social anthropology is a useful tool for the study of history has continued to be the subject of debate.[8] Modern readers of Thomas's work are presented with numerous examples of this method in practice, which will help them to form their own opinions.

In addition to its argument and methodology, *Religion* presents a wealth of primary source material, much of which had never been studied before its publication and which is still unparalleled in scope for this period and subject. Even if Thomas's central thesis were to be entirely rejected, his mastery of these sources and his discussion of their potential for understanding sixteenth- and seventeenth-century England would remain unquestioned. To put it simply, *Religion* would be valuable for its footnotes alone.

NOTES

1 Peter Burke, "Keith Thomas," in *Civil Histories: Essays Presented to Sir Keith Thomas*, ed. Peter Burke et al. (Oxford: Oxford University Press, 2000), 1–30.

2 Burke, "Keith Thomas," 9.

3 H. C. Erik Midelfort, "Review: *Religion and the Decline of Magic," Journal of the American Academy of Religion* 41 (1973): 432.

4 See Academy of Arts and Sciences, "Hundred Most Influential Books Since the War," *Bulletin of the American Academy of Arts and Sciences* 49 (1996): 12–18.

5 Burke, "Keith Thomas," 18.

6 Keith Thomas, *Religion and the Decline of Magic: Studies in Popular Beliefs in Sixteenth- and Seventeenth-Century England* (London: Penguin, 1991), 247–50.

7 Thomas, *Religion*, 402.

8 See, for example, the debate in the 1990s that took place between the anthropologists Marshall Sahlins and Gananath Obeyesekere regarding the rationality of indigenous peoples: Gananath Obeyesekere, *The Apotheosis Of Captain Cook: European Mythmaking In The Pacific* (Princeton: Princeton University Press, 1992); Marshall Sahlins, *How "Natives" Think: About Captain Cook, For Example* (Chicago: University of Chicago Press, 1995).

SECTION 1
INFLUENCES

MODULE 1
THE AUTHOR AND THE HISTORICAL CONTEXT

KEY POINTS

- *Religion and the Decline of Magic* provides a wealth of material about popular early modern* attitudes to witches,* fairies, magic,* and the supernatural, and suggests how these attitudes changed over the sixteenth and seventeenth centuries.

- Postwar Britain saw both a flourishing of new forms of social history* and a willingness to borrow useful models from the social sciences.

- Keith Thomas was based in Oxford, where he was exposed to other social historians—notably the influence of his teacher, the Marxist* Christopher Hill.*

Why Read this Text?

First published in 1971, *Religion* examines the complex relationship between magic, religion, and science in England in the sixteenth and seventeenth centuries. In the work, Keith Thomas proposes that this period saw a decline in magical belief and superstition and examines the factors that contributed to this decline.

The text is important for its novel approach to social history. While it was usual practice in historical research to focus on elite religious and intellectual culture, Thomas directed his research to popular belief. To do this, he examined very diverse, previously neglected and underused sources such as the notebooks of astrologers* and medical practitioners, the records of the ecclesiastical (Christian* Church) courts, and literary works. In doing this, Thomas pioneered a method

> 66 This book began as an attempt to make sense of the systems of belief which were current in sixteenth- and seventeenth-century England, but which no longer enjoy much recognition today. Astrology,* witchcraft, magical healing, divination,* ancient prophecies, ghosts and fairies, are now all rightly disdained by intelligent persons. But they were taken seriously by equally intelligent persons in the past, and it is the historian's business to explain why this was so. 99
>
> Keith Thomas, *Religion and the Decline of Magic*

of historical research that drew heavily on the work of social anthropologists* such as E. E. Evans-Pritchard,* whose studies on African witchcraft,* Thomas believed, could inform our understanding of early modern magical belief and practice.

The work has proved to be enormously influential as a model for historical research. Although the value of social anthropology as a historical tool has since been contested, Thomas is still credited with having opened up new areas of research in the field of popular religion and belief. *Religion* continues to be widely read by academics, students, and the general public.

Author's Life

Keith Thomas was born in 1933 in a small Welsh village and spent his early years in one of the most remote parts of Britain.[1] His understanding of the dynamics of rural communities in his writing about village witchcraft, for example, may owe something to this experience.

Thomas was born to Protestant* Christians. His mother lost her faith after the death of a daughter, while his father remained a churchgoer.[2] By the time he was an adult, Thomas, too, no longer believed in God.[3] Today, he is one of the patrons of the British Humanist Association,* an organization that represents nonreligious people committed to the advancement of ethical life.[4]

Although he has not discussed the reasons for his loss of faith in his writing, the measured, detached tone of his descriptions of religious or popular beliefs perhaps suggests that Thomas's world view has shaped his research.

Thomas joined Balliol College at Oxford University in 1952 and was to remain at Oxford for all of his academic career. His main influence as a student and early career academic was his mentor Christopher Hill, a Marxist who created the Communist Party Historians Group* and who helped to found *Past and Present*,* an innovative history journal that showcased a lot of new history writing.

If Thomas owed a great deal to Hill, and indeed later helped to edit *Past and Present*,[5] he did not share his Marxist historical approach. Thomas was ambitious for social history in its own right, believing that, since it could reveal patterns of thought that political or institutional history could not, it could answer important general questions about civilization.

In writing *Religion*, Thomas was also influenced by the interdisciplinary culture of postwar Oxford, according to which a researcher would draw on the research methods of different disciplines (that is, fields of study) for the benefit of his or her work. In the 1960s he began to read social anthropology extensively and came into contact with E. E. Evans-Pritchard and other world-leading Oxford anthropologists, eventually even reading papers at the Social Anthropology faculty.[6]

Author's Background

Although British scholars had come to social history later than their peers in the United States and on the European mainland, the focus on social history and popular belief Thomas displayed in *Religion* was becoming more typical in Britain in the 1960s and the early 1970s.[7]

This growing interest in social history depended, to a degree, on changes in contemporary British society. The 1960s had, after all, seen the development of a more "progressive" Britain. There had been the second postwar Labour* administration, the further decline of the British Empire* and a partial loosening of the rigid social order. Perhaps reflecting this, Thomas's work focused on a period of radical change in England—Scotland, Ireland, and Wales were for the most part excluded from *Religion*—that saw widespread instability as a result of the sixteenth-century English Reformation,* a time of great religious upheaval, and the English Civil War (1642–51).*

Thomas's interest in magic and popular religion chimed with contemporary interests in alternative forms of spirituality. In addition, his extensive use of social anthropology, with frequent references to developing cultures, made the book of particular interest in an increasingly multicultural society.

NOTES

1   Peter Burke, "Keith Thomas," in *Civil Histories: Essays Presented to Sir Keith Thomas*, ed. Peter Burke et al. (Oxford: Oxford University Press, 2000), 2.

2   Alan Macfarlane, "Interview of Sir Keith Thomas—On His Life and Work (September 5, 2009)," accessed September 14, 2013, http://www.sms.cam.ac.uk/media/1132829.

3   Macfarlane, "Interview."

4   British Humanist Association, "Sir Keith Thomas M.A., F.B.A.," accessed February 12, 2015, https://humanism.org.uk/about/our-people/patrons/sir-keith-thomas/.

5   Burke, "Keith Thomas," 15.
    Burke, "Keith Thomas," 22–30.
    Burke, "Keith Thomas," 23.

6   Macfarlane, "Interview of Sir Keith Thomas."

7   Adrian Wilson, "A Critical Portrait Of Social History," in *Rethinking Social History: English Society 1570–1920 and its Interpretation*, ed. Adrian Wilson (Manchester: Manchester University Press, 1993), 16.

ACADEMIC CONTEXT

KEY POINTS

- The field of early modern* history (about 1500–1700) was dominated by studies of the ways the English Protestant Reformation* in the early part of the sixteenth century changed broader patterns of belief. Religious change had traditionally been studied through Church history or the history of politics.

- Keith Thomas wanted to approach religion from the perspective of ordinary individuals—that is, through social history.* He also borrowed insights from other disciplines, notably social anthropology.*

- Thomas was bold in giving credibility to and rigorously analyzing sources from outside political or institutional history, such as those that dealt with superstitious beliefs and practices.

The Work in Its Context

The key question of *Religion and the Decline of Magic*—the reasons behind the decline in magical* thinking in England during the early modern period—places the work in the field of religious and intellectual history.* One of the main concerns of this field has been the study of the concept of rationality.

Since the Enlightenment,* a seventeenth-century movement favoring "reason" over religion and superstition, there had been a belief in the West that a more rational way of living (frequently associated with the Reformation) had replaced an older "superstitious" way of life (frequently associated with medieval and early modern Roman Catholicism).*

> ❝ By juxtaposing [religion] to the other, less esteemed systems of belief, I hope to have thrown more light on both, and to have contributed to our knowledge of the mental climate of early modern England. I have also tried to explore the relationship between this climate and the material environment more generally. ❞
>
> Keith Thomas, *Religion and the Decline of Magic*

This idea was itself associated with the celebrated and pioneering German sociologist Max Weber★ (1864–1920), who looked at the question in relation to the rise of Protestantism and labeled modern demystification★ "disenchantment with the world" (*Entzauberung der Welt*).[1]

The methodological approach adopted by Thomas in *Religion* reflects other developments in the field of social history. One of the most notable movements in twentieth-century historiography (the writing of history, and the study of writing on history) was the Annales school,* a group of French historians including Lucien Febvre* and Marc Bloch.* The historians associated with this movement, who dominated the field of social history in the post-World War II* years, rejected history that concentrated on political institutions in favor of a focus on broad social and cultural changes. Bloch, in particular, pioneered both the application of anthropology to historical source materials, and the study of past mentalities* (that is, patterns of thought—the "mind of the time").

Overview of the Field

Before *Religion* was published in 1971, studies had focused on the place of magic in intellectual and philosophical history. The work of historian Lynn Thorndike* on the history of magic and science concentrated largely on magical theory rather than practice, for example. Thomas's reaction to this, in trying to present an account of popular beliefs and traditions, may be seen as part of a wider movement in the field of history that had been taking place in England since the 1950s. This was the development of "history from below," an approach influenced by Marxist* thought that focused on the experiences of ordinary people.

Although he does not explicitly acknowledge this in the work, Thomas's approach to the subjects of magic and religion, viewing both of them from a cultural rather than a theological* perspective, owes much to the anthropologist James Frazer's* key work *The Golden Bough* of 1890. The first anthropological text to undertake a wide-ranging comparative study of religion, myth, and science, *The Golden Bough* caused controversy when it was published because the author decided to consider Christian* theology using the same criteria he applied to popular folk beliefs and pagan myth. It found a wide readership, nevertheless, and was a lasting influence on both academia and the arts.

Academic Influences

Thomas was influenced by a number of his immediate colleagues and students during his time at Oxford—in particular, the circle of socialist and Marxist historians surrounding his mentor Christopher Hill.* The writings of Marx had always been an important influence on social history, but the Communist Party Historians Group,* founded in 1946 and including Hill and other prominent historians such as E. P. Thompson* and Eric Hobsbawm,* was the first organization of its kind. Although Thomas clearly shared this group's interest in social history, he seemed to reject Marxism in his writings. His work displays little interest in economic history, for example, or class-based analysis.[2]

Perhaps the most direct influence on *Religion* might be said to have come from Alan Macfarlane*—one of Thomas's own students whose work was instrumental in the writing of the chapters on witchcraft.*

Thomas acknowledged the value of his discussions with Macfarlane in the book's introduction and made use of the data collected from Macfarlane's doctorate. Some have gone so far as to talk of the "Thomas–Macfarlane" thesis on witchcraft as a result.[3]

In his approach to social history Thomas adopted an interdisciplinary method that drew in particular on social anthropology. His main influence in this respect was the work of E. E. Evans-Pritchard,* who had given a significant lecture at Oxford in 1961 arguing that history and anthropology were almost identical disciplines.[4] Thomas believed that Evans-Pritchard's study of magic in contemporary societies could inform the historian's analysis of magical practices in the past.

Another key influence was the work of the Polish anthropologist Bronislaw Malinowski,* who had argued that magical practices needed to be analyzed in the context of their aims. This idea was to be integral to Thomas's explanation of the purpose of early modern magical thinking.

NOTES

1 Translated as "elimination of magic from the world" in Max Weber, *The Protestant Ethic and the Spirit of Capitalism* (London: Allen and Unwin, 1930), 105.

2 Peter Burke, "Keith Thomas," in *Civil Histories: Essays Presented to Sir Keith Thomas*, ed. Peter Burke et al. (Oxford: Oxford University Press, 2000), 9; 22–30.

3 Jonathan Barry, introduction to *Witchcraft in Early Modern Europe: Studies in Culture and Belief*, ed. J. Barry et al. (Cambridge: Cambridge University Press, 1996), 1–45.

4 Alan Macfarlane, "*Review of Keith Thomas, Religion and the Decline of Magic,*" *History Today* 31 (1981).

MODULE 3
THE PROBLEM

KEY POINTS

- *Religion and the Decline of Magic* tries to answer the question of to what extent "irrational" and magical* ways of thinking declined in England in the early modern period* between 1500 and 1700.

- Traditionalist historians like Hugh Trevor-Roper* believed changes in early modern thought happened because of political and institutional developments.

- Keith Thomas presented an alternative view, examining the problem using methods drawn from social history* and social anthropology* to explain the reasons behind magical belief.

Core Question

In the area Thomas chose to study, the history of popular religious and magical belief in England, the key questions were these: To what extent did a belief in magic decline during the early modern period, and what were the reasons behind this decline? Was the decline in magic a result of changes in conventional religious belief, or could it have been because of a rise in belief in science and "rational" thinking?

In the popular imagination, the Middle Ages* have long been associated with superstition and irrational, particularly supernatural, belief. The Protestant Reformation,* an upheaval in European religion in the early sixteenth century that saw great divisions between the Roman Catholic* and Protestant* churches, was seen as the first step towards the progressive "rationalization" of the Western world. The German sociologist Max Weber* described it as "disenchantment" (*Entzauberung*)[1]—a term he used to explain the progression of Western

> 66 The beliefs to which we must now turn were all
> conceived to explain misfortune and to mitigate its
> rigour. 99
>
> Keith Thomas, *Religion and the Decline of Magic*

society from superstition and mystical outlook towards secularization*
and scientific thinking. This development has been viewed as one of
the key elements of modernity.

The issue of the decline of magic is more complex, however, than
this thesis implies.

As Thomas's study reveals, the relationship between magic, religion,
and science has historically been difficult to define, and the boundaries
between these definitions are somewhat elastic. So the decline of
"magic" was not only difficult to prove but difficult to put down with
any certainty to either changes in religious practice or the development
of scientific thought.

The Participants

The study of magic and religion in the medieval and early modern
periods may be related to broader developments in historiography
(that is, the writing of history, and the study of writings on historical
subjects) that took place in the years after World War II.*

In the 1950s and the 1960s, British history writing had become a
battleground. On the one side there were traditionalists like Geoffrey
Elton* and Hugh Trevor-Roper*—historians who favored a "top-
down" approach to historical change that emphasized the importance
of political and religious institutions. On the other side there were
those who, under the influence of social theories like Marxism,*
attempted to recreate the lives of ordinary people. The latter group
included Thomas's supervisor at Oxford, Christopher Hill,* and other
historians associated with the Communist Party Historians Group.*

As one of the supporters of the traditional approach, Trevor-Roper argued in his work *The European Witch Craze of the Sixteenth and Seventeenth Centuries* that the belief system behind the witch-hunts* of the early modern period was the creation of the Church authorities, and not an indication of actual folk tradition or practice regarding magic.[2] According to this argument, the evidence from sources relating to witch trials could not be taken to be evidence of actual beliefs about witches, as confessions were extracted under torture. By minimizing the role of popular belief in witch trials, Trevor-Roper presented a view that gave more weight to the role of the intellectual elite.

The Contemporary Debate

In *Religion*, Thomas both built on and challenged the theories put forward by previous scholars. Although he used Max Weber's theory of "disenchantment" as a model for changing popular belief, he departed from it in some respects, being less confident than Weber about the generalized move towards reason.

Thomas found that, while beliefs in magic declined in England over the period of his study, they did so in different ways and at different speeds in different areas. Further, and again somewhat at odds with Weber, he did not believe that Protestantism played a central role in the decline in magical belief.[3]

As a supporter of social history, Thomas examined magic from a different perspective to contemporaries like Trevor-Roper. Rather than looking at witchcraft* from "above," as Trevor-Roper had, Thomas looked at it from "below"—from the level of the village rather than the Church. In doing this, Thomas benefited from his extensive readings in social anthropology, a field in which witchcraft was discussed a lot.

Thomas looked for patterns behind accusations of witchcraft, asking how these accusations might have "worked" for sixteenth- and seventeenth-century English villagers. His argument was that the execution of witches was seen as necessary because the magical protection of the Catholic Church had been removed by the growing influence of Protestantism.[4] He also examined the psychological and sociological elements behind these accusations, discussing the fact that people identified as witches tended to be women who had been begging for food or for money from neighbors of a higher social class.[5]

NOTES

1   Translated as "elimination of magic from the world" in Max Weber, *The Protestant Ethic and the Spirit of Capitalism* (London: Allen and Unwin, 1930), 105.

2   Hugh Trevor-Roper, *The European Witch Craze of the Sixteenth and Seventeenth Centuries* (London: Penguin, 1969).

3   Keith Thomas, *Religion and the Decline of Magic: Studies in Popular Beliefs in Sixteenth and Seventeenth-Century England* (London: Penguin, 1991), 755–800.

4   Thomas, *Religion*, 588–98.

5   Thomas, *Religion*, 599–611.

MODULE 4
THE AUTHOR'S CONTRIBUTION

KEY POINTS

- Original in the depth of its scope, *Religion* examines subjects that had previously not been considered fit for academic study.

- Thomas adopted a new approach inspired by movements in the field of social history.* The book's value came less from the fixed answers it provided than from the questions it asked and the sources it explored.

- Thomas argued that magical* thinking was not irrational but had proper practical effectiveness

Author's Aims

Keith Thomas set out his core aims in his title—*Religion and the Decline of Magic: Studies in Popular Beliefs in Sixteenth- and Seventeenth-Century England*. He hoped to establish that the use of magic declined in the years 1500 to 1700 or thereabouts, and to connect that decline to religious changes in England, particularly the English Reformation* and the Enlightenment,* and to other social developments such as the rise of science.

Although this was not a new subject, no one had previously approached it on such a large scale. Thomas attempted to cover all areas of popular belief, from popular Christianity* to ghosts, by way of fairies and witchcraft.* While some of these topics had been studied before, witchcraft among them, Thomas was a pioneer in giving scholarly attention to historical attitudes towards fairies, prophecy,* and astrology.*

> ❝ The medieval church thus appeared as a vast reservoir of magical power, capable of being deployed for a variety of secular purposes. Indeed it is difficult to think of any human aspiration for which it did not cater. Almost any object associated with ecclesiastical ritual could assume a special aura in the eyes of the people. ❞
>
> Keith Thomas, *Religion and the Decline of Magic*

Although the study of history from the perspective of ordinary individuals was increasingly accepted as a valid subject for research in Britain, in 1971 there was still a tendency to view the study of witchcraft and folklore as less valuable than the history of "learned" magic, broadly referring to those types of magic involving written materials and practiced by a literate elite.

Thomas had two broad aims: to rethink the parameters in which popular belief in early modern* European history was discussed and to start a debate about the nature of the study of popular belief as a historical issue.

By establishing the decline of magic as a historical "problem" requiring a solution, Thomas hoped both to assess the impact of magic and explain its appeal. Indeed, he summarizes his task as the need to "offer a *psychological* explanation of the motives of the participants in the drama of witchcraft accusation, a *sociological* analysis of the situation in which such accusations tended to occur and an *intellectual* explanation of the concepts which made such accusations plausible."[1]

Approach

Thomas's unique approach came from his attitude to the beliefs he studied. Whereas previous accounts of popular magic might have either sensationalized or looked down on it, Thomas attempted to understand the thinking that lay behind these beliefs. "Astrology, witchcraft, magical healing, divination,* ancient prophecies, ghosts and fairies, are now all rightly disdained by intelligent persons. But they were taken seriously by equally intelligent persons in the past, and it is the historian's business to explain why this was so."[2]

Thomas's view was that people in the premodern era were "equally intelligent," despite their apparently irrational beliefs. In this he was influenced by movements in the field of social history that had increasingly come to focus on the mentality and culture of groups outside the social elite.

Thomas's approach was primarily empirical* rather than theoretical—that is, he gathered large amounts of primary source material and made his case through example and counterexample rather than through more abstract social and cultural analysis. It is worth noting, however, that he regretted the unevenness of his sources, because they did not allow him to undertake a more thorough statistical analysis. The book was, as he later admitted, "essentially descriptive"[3] or even "an ethnography"*—a scientific description of peoples, cultures, and habits.[4]

Thomas aimed to chart the phenomenon of the decline of magic, recognizing that it would be difficult to establish any firm conclusions as to *why* it was collapsing. If the conclusions he does make are tentative rather than dogmatic, this has proved to be a strength. Because the book's fate was not totally bound up with its arguments, he guaranteed the work's longevity.

By asking a series of open-ended questions, *Religion* remains the starting point for almost any attempt to chart shifts in culture and thought in early modern England. It is also a demonstration that in history, asking the right question is often more important than giving a fashionable but temporary answer.

Contribution in Context

In *Religion*, Thomas argues that although magic was condemned by Christian doctrine, the Roman Catholic Church* had effectively encouraged magical practices with, say, priests blessing crops. After the rise of Protestantism* following the English Reformation,* Church authorities tried to suppress such practices. Magical tradition survived in rural areas before gradually dying away as a result of the rise in scientific belief.

The idea that there had been a crossover between magical and religious practice was something that had been raised in earlier scholarship.[5] Prior to Thomas, however, no one had either attempted such a comprehensive account or attempted to explain why this crossover might have existed.

Thomas's answer to this question of the decline of magic came from his social anthropological* approach. Drawing on the work of the Polish anthropologist Bronislaw Malinowski,* he aimed to discover the "practical utility" of magical practices.[6] In line with Malinowski's argument, Thomas claimed that "the most important cause of man's recourse to magic is his lack of the necessary empirical or technical knowledge to deal with the problems which confront him."[7] As people became increasingly able to solve these problems on the back of scientific and technological developments, magic became less important. "The decline of magic coincided with a marked improvement in the extent to which [man's] environment became amenable to control."[8]

The use of social anthropology* as an analytical tool for historical sources was not in itself a new idea. The French historian Marc Bloch,* for instance, was influenced by anthropology in his important examination of medieval beliefs about the healing power of kings, *Les rois thaumaturges* (1924, translated as *The Royal Touch* in 1973).[9] However, the originality of Thomas's approach lay in its broad application. Rather than using anthropology to explain one particular magical belief, he attempted to develop an explanation for an entire belief system.

NOTES

1 Keith Thomas, *Religion and the Decline of Magic: Studies in Popular Beliefs in Sixteenth- and Seventeenth-Century England* (London: Penguin, 1991), 559.

2 Thomas, *Religion*, ix.

3 Alan Macfarlane, "Interview of Sir Keith Thomas—On His Life and Work (September 5, 2009)," accessed September 14, 2013, http://www.sms. cam.ac.uk/media/1132829.

4 Keith Thomas, "An Anthropology of Religion and Magic, II," *Journal of Interdisciplinary History* 6 (1975), 108.

5 See, for example, J. Edward Waugh, *Church Folklore: A Record of Some Post-Reformation Usages in the English Church, Now Mostly Obsolete* (London: Griffith Farran and Co., 1894).

6 Thomas, *Religion*, ix.

7 Thomas, *Religion*, 775.

8 Thomas, *Religion*, 777.

9 See Marc Bloch, *The Royal Touch: Sacred Monarchy and Scrofula in England and France* (London: Routledge and Kegan Paul, 1973).

SECTION 2
IDEAS

KEY POINTS

- Thomas approaches his subject through seven themes: religion, magic,* witchcraft,* fairies and supernatural creatures, astrology,* prophecy,* and "omens and the calendar."

- Thomas argues that in early modern* society between around 1500 and 1700, magic performed a function that was gradually replaced by religion and science. But this process did not happen in any uniform or predictable way.

- *Religion*'s thematic structure proved to be both an advantage and a disadvantage, but its overall effectiveness is rarely disputed.

Key Themes

Keith Thomas's *Religion and the Decline of Magic* is concerned with the decline of magical ways of thinking in England between about 1500 and 1700.

Thomas examines those ways of thinking through the four major themes of religion, magic, astrology, and witchcraft, and the three subsidiary themes of fairies and ghosts, prophecy, and "omens and the calendar."

Addressing these themes, however, and the ways in which the strength of the magical beliefs behind them changed over time, Thomas faced a problem. Although each theme was important to his thesis, the evidence he needed to back up his arguments varied greatly in both quality and quantity.

It is more difficult to research a subject when primary sources—testimony and first-hand accounts, for example—are thin. As "witches"

> ❝ The beliefs with which this book is concerned had a variety of social and intellectual implications. But one of their central features was a preoccupation with the explanation and relief of human misfortune. ❞
>
> Keith Thomas, *Religion and the Decline of Magic*

left no testimony behind apart from court records,[1] Thomas found some important works on the subject of witchcraft, but no developed tradition of research. Meanwhile, a great deal had been written on late medieval and early modern Christian* belief—but not on the subject of prophecy. Thomas essentially pioneered historical work in a field where few historians of early modern England had gone before. But he was forced to treat these subjects somewhat unevenly.

Exploring the Ideas

Thomas's main argument is that, in the early modern period, magic served a practical function. Magical beliefs and actions were designed to fix problems for which an unstable society had not yet produced solutions. Before a modern understanding of the function of the human body and the causes of disease, for example, magical treatments provided an alternative. And, as Thomas explains, they were sometimes effective for psychological reasons.

An examination of one of Thomas's key themes, witchcraft, reveals the complex relationship between magic and religion.

Thomas explains that the medieval Church offered much in the way of magical protection to the members of its community: "Holy water,* the sign of the cross, holy candles, church bells, consecrated* herbs, sacred words worn next to the body were the means through which the Christian might secure immunity from the fiend."[2] Thomas argues that these practices were "magical" because the items were popularly believed to be effective in their own right. In other words, they did not depend on the faith of the individual.

With the English Reformation,* the schism in the Church that saw Protestant* doctrine become more popular than Roman Catholicism* in many European countries, the Church attempted to stamp out these beliefs. Instead it emphasized the importance of more traditional practices such as prayer, fasting, and the leading of a Christian life. But the Church did not deny that the devil was real or that his followers had the power to harm—which, as Thomas explains, proved problematic for many:

"Protestantism forced its adherents into the intolerable position of asserting the reality of witchcraft, yet denying the existence of an effective and legitimate form of protection or cure. The Church of England discarded the apparatus of mechanical religious formulae, but it was not prepared to claim that faith alone would protect the godly from witchcraft."[3]

Deprived of the magical elements of Christian faith, people turned towards popular folk magic as a means of protection. So while the Reformation prompted a movement away from magical belief generally, in certain respects it also caused a turn towards it.

The most obvious effect of this process, Thomas argues, was the increase in the persecution of witches by the community and the authorities and the widespread witch-hunts* of the seventeenth century. "Religion offered no certain immunity; counter-magic was prohibited. The ultimate onus of checking the damage done by witchcraft thus fell on the courts, and the legal prosecution of the witch became the one sure way out of what was otherwise a total *impasse*."[4]

Language and Expression

Thomas intended the work to appeal to both an academic and a general readership, so he writes in a clear, accessible style. The subject matter requires a degree of specialist vocabulary and Latin terms, but he is careful to explain them. Thomas's attitude towards academic writing may be summarized by his advice to his then-student, Alan Macfarlane.* "Everything must be clear, unpretentious, without jargon or complication."[5] The book also begins with an extensive introduction for the reader unfamiliar with the context of early modern English society.

The thematic structure of *Religion* has both positive and negative aspects. On the one hand, its fragmented nature means those who want to research a particular topic in the field of magic can easily find the relevant section of the work. Indeed, having become a historian and social anthropologist himself, Alan Macfarlane went so far as to describe *Religion* as "four short books" on religion, magic, astrology, and witchcraft, combined with a series of longer essays on ancient prophecies, ghosts and fairies, and times and omens.[6] Each of the book-length studies can stand, to some extent, on its own. The proof of this is that those parts dealing with magic and witchcraft have been translated into Italian and German respectively, without reference to the rest of the book.[7] But the thematic organization does not, perhaps, serve the clarity of the book's themes or the author's overarching argument.

Although Thomas does give definitions for the key concepts of "religion" and "magic," he later regretted that he had not made the differences between those definitions clear enough.[8] Further, although the different themes support one another, they are so close in subject that there is an unavoidable overlap of material and discussion. The topic of cunning men and women appear in one guise under "magic," for example, and then under another in "witchcraft."[9]

Again, this demonstrates the problems Thomas faced in forming the subject's concepts and definitions: although he attempted to use only terms that had been current in the early modern period, he was later criticized for including some contemporary language that didn't exist at the time.[10]

NOTES

1   Keith Thomas, *Religion and the Decline of Magic: Studies in Popular Beliefs in Sixteenth- and Seventeenth-Century England* (London: Penguin, 1991), 27–206.

2   Thomas, *Religion*, 588.

3   Thomas, *Religion*, 590.

4   Thomas, *Religion*, 593.

5   Alan Macfarlane, "Review of Keith Thomas, *Religion and the Decline of Magic*," *History Today* 31 (1981).

6   Macfarlane, Review, *History Today* 31 (1981).

7   Giles Mandelbrote, "The Published Writings of Keith Thomas, 1957–1998," in *Civil Histories: Essays Presented to Sir Keith Thomas*, ed. Peter Burke et al. (Oxford: Oxford University Press, 2000), 359–377.

8   Keith Thomas, "An Anthropology of Religion and Magic, II," *Journal of Interdisciplinary History* 6 (1975): 95–8.

9   Thomas, *Religion*, 252–300.

10 Hildred Geertz, "An Anthropology of Religion and Magic, I," *Journal of Interdisciplinary History* 6, no. 1 (1975): 71–89.

MODULE 6
SECONDARY IDEAS

KEY POINTS

- For much of the early modern* period, the practices of magic* and science were related.
- With the dawn of the scientific revolution* in the 1500s—a current of rational and scientific thought that marked European culture increasingly deeply—the world view that sustained magic became unsupportable.
- Thomas paid less attention to the study of some aspects of magical thinking because evidence was scarce.

Other Ideas

In *Religion and the Decline of Magic* Keith Thomas describes how there was a substantial overlap between magic and science for much of the early modern period. For the uneducated, the methods of the doctor and the magical practitioner were equally obscure. "All the evidence of the sixteenth and seventeenth centuries suggests that the common people never formulated a distinction between magic and medicine."[1]

Furthermore, Thomas explains how many advances in science actually came about as the result of magical experimentation. These included such discoveries as heliocentrism (the fact that the Earth revolves around the Sun), the existence of the solar system,* the theory of blood circulation, and the movement of the celestial bodies* such as the Sun, the Moon, and the planets.

Thomas argues that this was due to a shared mind-set, necessary for both magical and scientific experimentation, which separated itself from the fatalistic* attitude common to medieval thought, that all human endeavor is subject to a preordained course of events. Although

> ❝ This union of magic and science was short-lived …
> The triumph of the mechanical philosophy meant the
> end of the animistic conception of the universe which
> had constituted the basic rationale for magical thinking. ❞
>
> Keith Thomas, *Religion and the Decline of Magic*

"magic and science had originally advanced side by side," he writes, the "magical desire for power had created an intellectual environment favorable to experiment and induction" that "marked a break with the characteristic medieval attitude of contemplative resignation."[2]

Thomas's study of astrology,* in particular, demonstrates the blurring of the lines between magic and science.

Astrology as a learned magic—that is, as something that is not intuitive, but more like a scholarly discipline—could only be practiced by the literate and educated. Its practitioners had to know the basics of astronomy* and mathematics to make their predictions and because of the nature of the problems people brought to them, they often doubled as medical practitioners.

Exploring the Ideas

Despite astrology's close relationship with science and the difference between it and other forms of more popular magic, Thomas still emphasizes its essentially magical nature. "Up to a point, of course, astrology was a different type of activity from the magic of the village wizards. It had an elaborate theoretical basis and appealed to educated persons … Nevertheless, the basic ingredients of astrological practice were much the same as those of the village wizard: lost goods, missing persons, sickness and disease. It is doubtful whether many clients saw any difference between the two types of practitioner."[3]

Thomas describes how, for this reason, belief in astrology declined in the early modern period along with other magical practices. By the early seventeenth century the developments associated with the scientific revolution had served to undermine magical thinking. Thomas argues that the key to this intellectual shift is "the triumph of the mechanical philosophy."[4] This school of thought viewed the world as if it were a machine, governed by laws and principles that could be predicted, and immune from the intervention of outside forces such as God or the devil.

According to Thomas, many of the discoveries made by these "mechanical philosophers" overturned the principles on which magic was based. The invention of the telescope, for example, and the subsequent discovery of previously unobserved stars, called into question all previous astrological knowledge. In addition, mechanical philosophy fostered a new empiricism*— that theories and assumptions be proved through rigorous testing. Magic, unable to meet this requirement, inevitably declined.

Thomas states, however, that these developments did not immediately filter down to the mass of uneducated people, who continued to a large extent with their magical beliefs: "These various developments thus robbed the old magical systems of their capacity to satisfy the educated élite. But it was to be some time before the people at large became fully aware of their implications."[5]

Overlooked

One of the subsidiary themes that Thomas addresses in his study of magical practice is the belief in supernatural beings—ghosts and fairies. Thomas's treatment of these topics, perhaps because of its comparative brevity, has attracted less interest in subsequent scholarship than his work on witchcraft* and astrology.

The scholarly study of ghosts was already established by the time Thomas wrote his work, because they were a crucial part of medieval Christian* eschatology,* the part of Christian teachings concerned with death.[6] The topic of fairies, however, remains less studied, at least in an early modern context. Thomas's treatment of the subject describes the contemporary belief in the essentially dangerous character of fairies. Early modern people turned to magic for protection from them in the same way that they looked for protection from illness and natural disasters. Thomas describes the difficulties in assessing the strength of these beliefs during any particular period because of the substantial differences in England's different regions.

As with his treatment of other magical beliefs, here Thomas's originality lies in the way he uses modern anthropological ideas and applies them to early modern contexts. He argues that a belief in fairies had a sociological function. In popular tradition fairies were said to punish people who were untidy, lazy, promiscuous, or disrespectful to their social superiors. "In such ways did fairy-beliefs help to reinforce some of the standards upon which the effective working of society depended."[7]

Another important aspect of Thomas's contribution to this topic lies in his research of archives. He examined a number of sources that had not previously been the subject of serious academic study and many subsequent works on the subject reference *Religion* rather than the original source material, much of which is still unedited.[8]

One recent work has offered a new perspective on Thomas's work on fairies. The British historian Emma Wilby* has argued that fairy belief and witchcraft were really just different sides of the same coin of belief. Fairies were "familiars," tame spirits under the command of cunning folk (that is, village sorcerers) and so witchcraft and fairies cannot be separated.[9]

NOTES

1   Keith Thomas, *Religion and the Decline of Magic: Studies in Popular Beliefs in Sixteenth- and Seventeenth-Century England* (London: Penguin, 1991), 800.

2   Thomas, *Religion*, 770.

3   Thomas, *Religion*, 760.

4   Thomas, *Religion*, 769.

5   Thomas, *Religion*, 772.

6   See, for example, J. H. Crehan, ed., *Ghosts and Poltergeists* (Chicago: Henry Regnery Co., 1954).

7   Thomas, *Religion*, 731–2

8   Regina Buccola, *Fairies, Fractious Women and the Old Faith* (Susquehanna: Susquehanna University Press, 2006), 246; Emma Wilby, *Cunning Folk and Familiar Spirits: Shamanistic Visionary Traditions in Early Modern British Witchcraft and Magic* (Eastbourne: Sussex Academic Press, 2005), 67, 90, 97, and 224.

9   Wilby, *Cunning Folk.*

MODULE 7
ACHIEVEMENT

KEY POINTS

- Thomas succeeded in throwing light on popular religious and magical* attitudes in England over two hundred years of transition. In doing so he showed the strengths of a research method that drew on both social history* and the social sciences generally.

- Although reactions to *Religion and the Decline of Magic* were generally positive, the way in which Thomas integrated social history and anthropology* in his work was criticized in some quarters.

- Some considered Thomas's anthropological model to be outdated; others argued that he failed to take continental sources into account.

Assessing the Argument

In *Religion and the Decline of Magic* Keith Thomas was generally successful in presenting a broad overview of the changing nature of magical belief in the early modern* period. His main achievements were twofold. First, he successfully used social history and other disciplines to tackle subjects that hadn't been studied up to that point. Second, he presented a lot of new primary source material on which future studies could be founded. Yet Thomas would have been the first to admit that in some respects his overall thesis was lacking.

The argument implicit in the work's title—that magic declined as a result of changes in religious practice—was a general trend, but it wasn't something that happened uniformly over two hundred years and across an entire country. So it was still possible to find examples to contradict this idea—for example, the growth in the belief that "the

> ❝ Today we think of religion as a belief, rather than a practice, as definable in terms of creeds rather than in modes of behaviour. But such a description would have fitted the popular Catholicism* of the Middle Ages* little better than it fits many other primitive religions. ❞
>
> Keith Thomas, *Religion and the Decline of Magic*

royal touch" could cure scrofula* (a form of tuberculosis) in the seventeenth century.[1]

Although the quality of Thomas's research was rarely in doubt, the problems with his main argument were highlighted by some when *Religion* was first published. One reviewer stated: "The only thing which prevents this book from being an unrelieved masterpiece is its conclusion, or rather, its lack of one … [Thomas] has very little to say about the "decline of magic" circa 1700 beyond rejecting some stock answers."[2]

Nevertheless, in the light of the breadth of his subject, this "failure" does not entirely undermine Thomas's achievement. His thesis was expressed tentatively, in the spirit of experiment—and as one reviewer put it, regarding the complex topics of magic and religion, "Keith Thomas is far too intelligent to propound final solutions."[3]

Achievement in Context

Although *Religion* was met with general critical acclaim when it was first published in 1971, in some respects it went against the approach adopted by more traditional historians. As a result the book was criticized in some quarters. This criticism mainly centered on Thomas's decision to adopt an interdisciplinary* methodology, in particular using concepts and theories from social anthropology.* This even made him the object of ridicule. Some staff members at Oxford University referred to him as "Bonga Bonga Thomas" in the 1970s.[4]

Other academic colleagues, however, were enthusiastic about Thomas's support for social history and interdisciplinary research. Christopher Hill* and other members of the Communist Party Historians Group* supported Thomas's aim of presenting an overview of popular, rather than elite, belief. This aim was in keeping with the principles of the new "history from below," which examined history from the perspective of groups and individuals from all social classes.

The main obstacle Thomas faced during his research was the comparative lack of published source material in certain areas. This meant he couldn't do any form of statistical analysis, which made it difficult for him to present ideas founded on hard data, and he had to adopt a more anecdotal style. Thomas felt this particularly keenly in an age when the birth of digital technology was just beginning to open up new possibilities for academic research:

"I particularly regret not having been able to offer more of those exact statistical data upon which the precise analysis of historical change must so often depend … In my attempt to sketch the main outlines of the subject I have only too often had to fall back upon the historian's traditional method of presentation by example and counter-example. Although this technique has some advantages, the computer has made it the intellectual equivalent of the bow and arrow in a nuclear age."[5]

Limitations

One of Thomas's achievements in *Religion* is to make the early modern period accessible by explaining its concepts in modern terms. His use of psychological terms to explain magical beliefs allows the modern reader to grasp the early modern mindset more fully. He also makes use of analogies, for instance comparing the reaction of an uneducated early modern person to magical and medical remedies to the "modern working-class woman who says she doesn't 'believe' in doctors."[6]

While this particular analogy might be seen as class prejudice, these methods may serve to make the book appealing to a wider audience.

"An exercise in comparative history, however desirable, is not possible until the data for each country have been properly assembled," wrote Thomas. Yet despite this assertion, *Religion* was also criticized for its failure to take continental sources into account.[7] This was, in the opinion of one reviewer, a major flaw. The study was "too limited by Dr. Thomas's too insular concentration on English witchcraft* in a vacuum, without the slightest relation to the continental counterpart which in fact produced it," he wrote.[8]

Recent developments in the field of the history of witchcraft, however, show how Thomas's study can be broadly applied to different contexts. Previous approaches to witch-hunts* in early modern Europe had emphasized the importance of theoretical and legal frameworks rather than social conditions. But recent works have focused on the common social context from which both the English and European witch-hunts emerged.[9]

Religion has been very important in the discipline of history, but its influence on the other discipline that Thomas drew on, anthropology, has been more limited. This may be down to a number of factors.

First, the book was criticized in anthropological circles for failing to properly define its concepts or to formulate a consistent anthropological methodology.[10] Second, by the time the book was published in 1971 much of the anthropological theory adopted by Thomas had come under attack from new movements in the discipline, such as structuralism* (the theory that cultures are governed by underlying patterns and forces that interact in a larger system).[11] Although never explicitly defined, Thomas's work uses a broadly functionalist* approach. This is founded on the assumption that every human action is somehow required by the society that fosters it, an idea that is difficult to reconcile with structuralist theory.

NOTES

1   Keith Thomas, *Religion and the Decline of Magic: Studies in Popular Beliefs in Sixteenth- and Seventeenth-Century England* (London: Penguin, 1991), 227–42.

2   E. William Monter, "Review of Keith Thomas, *Religion and the Decline of Magic*," *Journal of Modern History* 44:2 (1972): 264.

3   Frances Yates, "Review of *Religion and the Decline of Magic*," *The British Journal for the History of Science* 6 (1972), 214.

4   Peter Burke, "Keith Thomas," in *Civil Histories: Essays Presented to Sir Keith Thomas*, ed. Peter Burke et al. (Oxford: Oxford University Press, 2000), 13.

5   Thomas, *Religion*, x.

6   Thomas, *Religion*, 800.

7   Thomas, *Religion*, x.

8   Rossell Hope Robbins, "Review of Keith Thomas, *Religion and the Decline of Magic*," *Renaissance Quarterly* 26: 1(1973): 71.

9   See, for example, Robin Briggs, *Witches and Neighbours: The Social and Cultural Context of European Witchcraft (Oxford: Wiley-Blackwell, 2002).*

10 Hildred Geertz, "An Anthropology of Religion and Magic, I," *Journal of Interdisciplinary History* 6 (1975): 71–89.

11 Alan Macfarlane, "Review of Keith Thomas, *Religion and the Decline of Magic*," *History Today* 31 (1981).

MODULE 8
PLACE IN THE AUTHOR'S WORK

KEY POINTS

- Although *Religion and the Decline of Magic* was Thomas's first book, it was the culmination of many years of research. Its methodology was born out of earlier articles where Thomas showed he was in favor of an interdisciplinary approach.

- Thomas's work has generally examined the social, intellectual, and cultural history of early modern* England, making use of other disciplines like social anthropology.*

- *Religion* remains Thomas's most important work. In the last three decades he has become increasingly active in university administration.

Positioning

Although *Religion and the Decline of Magic* was Keith Thomas's first book, it was preceded by several important articles that indicated the direction his research was to take. Three articles published in the 1960s and early 1970s, especially, gave an indication of his historical methodology.

In the influential article "History and Anthropology," published in the Oxford history journal *Past and Present** in 1963, Thomas discussed ways in which the field of anthropology could inform that of history.[1] In "The Tools and the Job," published in the *Times Literary Supplement* in April 1966, Thomas argued strongly that it was important for social history* to be founded on a knowledge of the social sciences.[2] In 1970, he published an article saying that research methods developed by anthropologists could be applied to the subject of magic.*[3] These views helped Thomas develop his approach in *Religion* and in his work that followed.

> 66 … one is impressed less with a sense of a new methodology [in *Religion*], than with the evidence of the extension of a traditional historical discipline into new areas of research. 99
>
> E. P. Thompson,* "Anthropology and the Discipline of Historical Context," *Midland History* 1

Before *Religion*, Thomas had published on subjects including political thought and women in early modern England.[4] His former student Alan Macfarlane* claimed that Thomas first became interested in the subject of magic in 1963, when he (Macfarlane) was beginning to work with him as a doctoral student.[5] Unsurprisingly for a work so wide-ranging, *Religion* represents the culmination of many years of research, despite being Thomas's first work of length on a single theme. Although he did not publish any other substantial work on the topic of magic, Thomas's later books *Man and the Natural World* (1983) and *The Ends of Life* (2009) were both broad works of social history focusing on the early modern world view.[6]

Integration

Throughout his career, Thomas centered his research around the same topic, the early modern period in England, but approached it from two different perspectives:

- From the perspective of social history—the branch of history that emphasizes social structures and the interaction of different groups in society, rather than affairs of state.
- From the perspective of intellectual history*—the discipline exploring the history of ideas and thought

Within this period, in addition to magic, he has examined topics as diverse as education, aging, and early modern views of the past.[7]

In *Man and the Natural World* (1983), Thomas examined changing attitudes toward animals and nature in the early modern period. As he had in *Religion*, Thomas here viewed this process as a gradual movement away from a mystical,* symbolic mentality toward a greater dependence on objectivity and "rational" thought. In his most recent work, *The Ends of Life*, he returned to a theme previously addressed in *Religion*: What were the goals and aspirations of early modern people and how did they go about achieving these?

From a methodological perspective Thomas's work is remarkably consistent and cohesive. This is not to say that he has never re-evaluated his historical method. In fact, he has continued to reflect on it.[8] Broadly, however, his major works are characterized by an interdisciplinary* approach and a continued emphasis on primary source material. Thomas himself has caricatured his style as "a relentless diet of quotations."[9]

More recently he has said he has become more open to the traditional approaches in history he once attacked—but this does not mean he has substantially altered his historical method. Rather, Thomas believes one historical approach is not necessarily preferable to another.[10]

Significance

Religion is considered to be Thomas's most important book and it is the one for which he is best known amongst both an academic and a general readership. Although some of its ideas have been challenged, it continues to be widely read, and is frequently found on undergraduate reading lists. If his subsequent work has been well received, it must be said that it has not had the same impact; *Man and the Natural World*, for example, was praised both for the author's opening up of an understudied field and for its perceptive analysis of a wide range of source material, but it is not generally considered to be a pioneering work.[11]

Thomas's most recent major book, *The Ends of Life,* has so far received a less enthusiastic reception than his earlier works.[12] This may be in part due to Thomas's academic career having declined somewhat since his seminal work of the 1970s and 1980s. If Thomas does not publish as frequently as he once did, it is perhaps on account of his increasing involvement in university administration. In 1986, for example, he became president of Corpus Christi College, Oxford, and he has sat on many committees, the British Economic and Social Research Council among them.[13]

This has led some to suggest that he failed to capitalize on his early academic promise. As D. J. Taylor wrote in his review of Keith Thomas's The Ends of Life in the British *Independent** newspaper of February 13, 2009, he "revolutionised the way in which early modern historians approached the sixteenth and early seventeenth centuries … Then, unaccountably, [he] cast it all aside for the life of an academic *haut fonctionnaire,* the presidency of an Oxford college and a finger in every bureaucratic pie worth the tasting."[14]

However, this view has not much damaged Thomas's academic reputation, and he continues to be seen as one of the most influential scholars in his field.

NOTES

1   Keith Thomas, "History and Anthropology," in *Past and Present* 24 (1963): 3–24.

2   Keith Thomas, "The Tools and the Job," *Times Literary Supplement* (April 7, 1966): 275–6.

3   Keith Thomas, "The Relevance of Social Anthropology to the Study of English Witchcraft," in *Witchcraft Confessions and Accusations*, ed. Mary T. Douglas (London, Tavistock Publications, 1970), 47–80.

4   Keith Thomas, "The Social Origins of Hobbes' Political Thought," in *Hobbes Studies*, ed. K. C. Brown (Basil Blackwell, 1965); "Women and the Civil War Sects," *Past and Present* 13 (1958): 42–62.

5   Alan Macfarlane, "Review of Keith Thomas, *Religion and the Decline of Magic,*" *History Today 31* (1981).

6   Keith Thomas, *Man and the Natural World: Changing Attitudes in England, 1500–1800* (Oxford: Oxford University Press, 1983); *The Ends of Life: Roads to Fulfilment in Early Modern England* (Oxford: Oxford University Press, 2009).

7   Keith Thomas, *Rule and Misrule in the Schools of Early Modern England* (Reading: University of Reading, 1976); *Age and Authority in Early Modern England* (London: British Academy, 1976); *The Perception of the Past in Early Modern England: The Creighton Trust Lecture 1983* (London: University of London, 1983).

8   Keith Thomas, "Ways of Doing Cultural History," in *Balans en perspectief van de Nederlandse cultuurgeschiedenis*, ed. Rik Sanders et al. (Amsterdam: Rodopi, 1991).

9   Thomas, The Ends of Life, 5.

10 Alan Macfarlane, "Interview of Sir Keith Thomas—on His Life and Work (September 5, 2009)," accessed September 14, 2013, http:/www.sms.cam.ac.uk/media/1132829.

11 David Spring, "Review of Keith Thomas, *Man and the Natural World,*" *The American Historical Review* 89: 3 (1984): 733–4.

12 Eamon Duffy, "Common Thoughts," *London Review of Books* 31 (July 2009): 18–19.

13 Peter Burke, "Keith Thomas," 27.

14 D. J. Taylor, "Review of Keith Thomas, *The Ends of Life,*" The *Independent*, February 13, 2009.

SECTION 3
IMPACT

MODULE 9
THE FIRST RESPONSES

KEY POINTS

- While *Religion and the Decline of Magic* was generally well received when first published, it was criticized in some quarters for perceived flaws in its methodology and argument.

- Thomas entered into a dialogue with the anthropologist Hildred Geertz,* who was critical of his method.

- *Religion* was never substantially revised and the initial criticisms still inform debate today.

Criticism

Keith Thomas's *Religion and the Decline of Magic* was regarded as a classic work from the moment it was first published in 1971. The book was uniformly recognized as an enormous achievement for the wide-ranging nature and depth of its research, and Thomas was also praised for having opened up discussion in areas largely ignored until that point. "No one has ever studied the subject [of magic] in such depth as Professor Thomas," wrote one reviewer, Frances Yates.*[1]

Yet a number of criticisms were leveled against it. In terms of methodology, Thomas was seen as failing to provide a comprehensive definition for the social phenomena he was examining. In other words, he failed to fully consider the meaning of such concepts as "religion" and "magic"* and their different implications in the early modern* period.[2] Scholars working in other disciplines also felt the book had limited uses outside the field of history. As the reviewer for the journal *Contemporary Sociology** said, the "sociologist will find the amount of historical anecdote excessive."[3] The same reviewer also criticized the

> ❝ Fundamental changes in historical interpretation fall into two distinct categories. Some historians advance new interpretations of the familiar central phenomena of the historical scene, while others direct our attention to the importance of problems hitherto regarded as peripheral to historical interests ... It is Mr. Thomas's achievement to have pioneered both sorts of advance. ❞
>
> Robert Ashton, "Review of Keith Thomas, *Religion and the Decline of Magic*," *The Economic History Review*

book on the grounds of cultural specificity: "The book is very British; perhaps greater familiarity with the American literature on peasant societies might have been useful at a few points." Anthropologists,* on the other hand, regretted Thomas's lack of a unified and coherent anthropological theory.[4]

Content-wise, several scholars either disagreed with aspects of Thomas's argument or felt he had omitted subjects that were integral to his main intent. The reviewer Rossell Hope Robbins* felt he underplayed the role of the established Church in orchestrating the witch trials of the sixteenth and seventeenth centuries.[5] The historian of early modern philosophy and mysticism* Frances Yates criticized the fact that Thomas's work made no mention of the Cabala,* the philosophical teachings that were the basis for many magical practices. Yates felt this was central to the study of magic in the early modern period.[6] Perhaps more fundamentally, some saw the book as flawed because it didn't have a coherent argument and was unable to answer many of the questions it posed.[7]

Responses

The overall response to the book was positive and it seems likely Thomas would have felt vindicated in his choice of subject and his historical approach.

It is also possible that he did not feel the need to respond to *Religion*'s critics because he anticipated potential criticisms in the book itself. In the foreword to the 1973 edition, two years after the work first appeared, Thomas wrote that he regretted the lack of statistical data on which to base his analysis, and the anecdotal (or unscientific) character of much of the book that resulted.[8] He did not pretend that his conclusions were anything other than tentative and often presented evidence that appeared to contradict his general argument about the decline of magic.[9]

Thomas did respond to critics to discuss the book's problems. In 1975, for example, he wrote a response to anthropologist Hildred Geertz's assessment of *Religion* in the *Journal of Interdisciplinary History*,* defending himself from the charges of historical anachronism (placing something in an incorrect time period) and of misusing anthropology in relation to history.[10] In this article, Thomas explained his approach, stating his belief that, through a wide survey of the historical sources, he had arrived at a definition of magic that functioned "as a convenient label for bracketing together a variety of specific practices which contemporaries usually associated together."[11]

Conflict and Consensus

In 1973, a second edition of *Religion* was issued in which, responding to recent publications, Thomas "corrected some errors, pruned a few extravagances and added a handful of additional references."[12] Although the book has gone through numerous reprints and has seen various changes in format since 1973, Thomas has never taken up the challenge of a third edition.

If it might seem unusual for such an important book to remain substantially unrevised, particularly when its author is still active in university life, we can perhaps put this down to Thomas's stated opinion that, even if the book has theoretical weaknesses, its substance—that is, the evidence it draws on to make its arguments—is still of value. "It is fair to say," Thomas writes, "that the main substance of *Religion and the Decline of Magic* is what anthropologists would call ethnography* rather than theory; and the ethnography at least is, I hope, reasonably sound … If I were to rewrite my field notes I think that I should probably now cast them into a slightly different conceptual framework. But that is something which the critical reader can easily do for himself."[13]

Even without further contributions from the two academics, the dialogue between Thomas and Geertz has continued to inform the debate on the relationship between history and anthropology, and how this can help our understanding of the concepts of magic and religion.[14]

NOTES

1   James Hitchcock, "Review of Keith Thomas, *Religion and the Decline of Magic*," *The Review of Politics* 34: 3 (1972): 426.

2   Hitchcock, "Review": 426.

3   Alexander Rysman, "Review of Keith Thomas, *Religion and the Decline of Magic*," *Contemporary Sociology* 4, no. 2 (1975): 114

4   Hildred Geertz, "An Anthropology of Religion and Magic, I," *Journal of Interdisciplinary History* 6 (1975): 71–89.

5   Rossell Hope Robbins, "Review of Keith Thomas, *Religion and the Decline of Magic*," *Renaissance Quarterly* 26, no. 1 (1973): 72.

6   Frances Yates, "Review of *Religion and the Decline of Magic*," *The British Journal for the History of Science* 6 (1972): 214.

7   E. William Monter, "Review of Keith Thomas, *Religion and the Decline of Magic*," *Journal of Modern History* 44, no. 2 (1972): 264.

8   Keith Thomas, *Religion and the Decline of Magic: Studies in Popular Beliefs in Sixteenth- and Seventeenth-Century England* (London: Penguin, 1991), x.

9   See, for example, Thomas, *Religion*, 227–42.

10 Keith Thomas, "An Anthropology of Religion and Magic, II," *Journal of Interdisciplinary History* 6 (1975), 91–109.

11 Thomas, "An Anthropology," 95.

12 Thomas, *Religion,* xi.

13 Thomas, "An Anthropology," 108–9.

14 J. H. M. Salmon, "Review: History Without Anthropology: A New Witchcraft Synthesis," *Journal of Interdisciplinary History* 19, no. 3 (1989): 482

MODULE 10
THE EVOLVING DEBATE

KEY POINTS

- Many of the historians associated with the "cultural turn"*— the movement in which historians turned from the study of politics and economics to the study of things like culture and language—drew on Thomas's work.

- If there is no recognized "school of thought" based on Thomas's work, his influence has certainly been felt by many scholars working in several fields.

- Many of those most influenced by Thomas are his former students. Perhaps the most important of these is the historical anthropologist Alan Macfarlane.*

Uses and Problems

Since its publication in 1971 a great number of scholars have reassessed the topics and questions that Keith Thomas raised in *Religion and the Decline of Magic*.

Perhaps the most important legacy of the book is its methodology. In many ways, the approach Thomas adopted—an examination of history from a broad social and cultural perspective—pre-empted movements that followed in historiography (writing on history). The most notable of these movements is the "cultural turn": a re-evaluation of historical practice that happened in the 1970s and 1980s. Here many historians moved from studying politics and economics in their work to looking more closely at culture and language. The cultural turn had itself evolved from the new field of social history,* something to which Thomas himself had actively contributed in the 1960s.

> **❝** [*Religion and the Decline of Magic*] is perhaps the most important contribution to our understanding of English cultural history and indeed English history *tout court*, published in the past generation.[1] **❞**
>
> Christopher Hill,* "Partial Historians and Total History"

The cultural turn did not simply mean a focus on the cultural aspects of a past society, although this was certainly one of its aims. Rather, it viewed what was produced culturally as having meaning and significance that was necessary to understand the past. In other words, a society's language, art, or literature could provide clues to the values and thoughts of the people belonging to that society.

Thomas's attempt to use anthropological and psychological theory to understand the motivations behind early modern* magical ritual* and belief fitted the broad aims of the cultural turn. Indeed, in the 1960s Thomas wrote of cultural history as the successor of social history.

Religion also showed how historians could use social history to open up areas of popular religious and spiritual belief that had hardly been examined up to that point. Those who have followed Thomas in his aims and methods—such as the influential historian of fifteenth- and sixteenth-century English Christianity,* Eamon Duffy*— worked in the space that Thomas had established, focusing on those rituals and practices of popular religious belief in England that formed the backdrop of the English Reformation* (a period of cultural and religious turmoil).[2]

Schools of Thought

Although a recognized "school of thought" has not grown up around Thomas's work, he remains a powerful influence on the field of witchcraft* studies and on social and cultural history in general.

Among Thomas's followers are those who have used his work on magic as a basis for further research into popular religious and spiritual belief. Additionally, there are those who have been influenced by his historical methodology—particularly his adoption of a broad social and cultural approach to history that draws on the theory of the social sciences and related disciplines.

In 1996, former students of Thomas, together with other witchcraft scholars, published a volume of essays to mark the 25th anniversary of *Religion*.[3] A contemporary review summarized this volume as "in part a critique of the gaps and flaws subsequent work has exposed in his account; in part a review of the small forest of literature which has sprung up around this topic, and in part a warm tribute to the dedicatee."[4] In this volume, the scope of Thomas's original project was extended to include European witchcraft and his original thesis regarding the decline of magic was re-examined.

The agreed view amongst the contributors was that the changes in the nature of magical beliefs and practices cannot be attributed to a single cause and should instead be viewed in terms of "a mosaic of small overlapping narratives."[5]

In Current Scholarship

Perhaps the most important of Thomas's successors is the historian and anthropologist Alan Macfarlane.

Macfarlane's doctoral research contributed to Thomas's discussion of witchcraft in *Religion* to such an extent that some even refer to these chapters as the "Thomas-Macfarlane witchcraft thesis."[6] More than any other scholar, Macfarlane has embraced Thomas's interdisciplinary* approach. He has even gone so far as to get a second doctorate in the discipline of anthropology and has conducted fieldwork in Nepal.[7] More recently, Macfarlane has reassessed Thomas's core thesis in *Religion*, reinterpreting the reasons behind the collapse of a magical way of thinking in early modern England.[8]

Peter Burke* is another historian who sees Keith Thomas as a major influence. Studying under Thomas at Oxford, Burke became interested in anthropology in particular and interdisciplinary studies more generally.[9] Since the late 1970s, Burke has been one of the leading champions of cultural history.[10] He has both spoken of Thomas's *Religion* as an example of an innovative study of a cultural area, and acknowledged Thomas's part in the creation of cultural history as a discipline.[11]

The study of the English Reformation is one area of research that owes a particular debt to Thomas. His social historical approach to the subject of religion has prompted research on the popular beliefs and practices that formed a background to this period. Euan Cameron,* for example, is a historian of the Reformation whose work examining religious thought of the time owes much to Thomas's work;[12] Cameron acknowledges this debt in his *Enchanted Europe: Superstition, Reason, and Religion 1250–1750*, published in 2010.[13]

NOTES

1   Christopher Hill, "Partial Historians and Total History," in *The Collected Essays of Christopher Hill: Volume Three, People and Ideas in Seventeenth-Century England* (Amherst: University of Massachusetts Press, 1986), 7.

2   Eamon Duffy, *The Stripping of the Altars: Traditional Religion in England 1400–1580* (New Haven and London: Yale University Press, 1992), 1.

3   Jonathan Barry et al., eds., *Witchcraft in Early Modern Europe: Studies in Culture and Belief* (Cambridge: Cambridge University Press, 1996).

4   Alexandra Walsham, "Review of *Witchcraft in Early Modern Europe*," *The English Historical Review* 451 (1998): 452.

5   Robin Briggs, "Many Reasons Why: Witchcraft and the Problem of Multiple Explanation," in *Witchcraft,* ed. Jonathan Barry et al., 63.

6   Jonathan Barry, introduction to *Witchcraft*, ed. Jonathan Barry et al., 2.

7   Adrian Wilson, "A Critical Portrait Of Social History," in *Rethinking Social History: English Society 1570–1920 and its Interpretation*, ed. Adrian Wilson (Manchester: Manchester University Press, 1993), 17.

8   Alan Macfarlane, "Civility and the Decline of Magic," in *Civil Histories: Essays Presented to Sir Keith Thomas*, ed. Peter Burke et al. (Oxford: Oxford University Press, 2000), 145–59.

9   Melissa Calaresu, "Introduction: Peter Burke and the History of Cultural History," in *Exploring Cultural History: Essays in Honour of Peter Burke*, ed. Melissa Calaresu et al. (Farnham: Ashgate, 2010), 12–14.

10 See, in particular, Peter Burke, *Popular Culture in Early Modern Europe* (London, 1978); *What is Cultural History?* (Cambridge, 2004).

11 "Interview with Peter Burke," in Ewa Domanska, *Encounters: Philosophy of History After Postmodernism* (Charlottesville: University Press of Virginia, 1998), 214–15; Keith Thomas, "Ways of Doing Cultural History," in *Balans en perspectief van de Nederlandse cultuurgeschiedenis*, ed. Rik Sanders et al. (Amsterdam: Rodopi, 1991).

12 Euan Cameron, *The European Reformation* (Oxford: Oxford University Press, 2012).

13 Euan Cameron, *Enchanted Europe: Superstition, Reason, and Religion 1250–1750* (Oxford: Oxford University Press, 2010), iii.

MODULE 11
IMPACT AND INFLUENCE TODAY

KEY POINTS

- *Religion and the Decline of Magic* is still considered a key text in its field. It has prompted debate in such key areas as the role of the Protestant* Reformation* in the rise of "reason" and the birth of modernity.

- The book continues to inform debate about the relationship between history and anthropology.

- Thomas's main argument about the decline of magic* remains a rich topic of discussion.

Position

Keith Thomas's *Religion and the Decline of Magic* is generally considered to be one of the most important works of historical scholarship of the second half of the twentieth century.[2] It has had an enormous influence on history writing since World War II,* both in pointing the way to new fields of study and in demonstrating an innovative historical approach.

Many contemporary scholars who cite the work use Thomas's extensive primary research to support their own arguments. Others engage more directly with specific aspects the book. American social historian* David Cressy,* for example, questions Thomas's explanation for the deliberate undermining of Christian* rituals such as baptism in the early modern* period. Cressy argues that such practices may be explained more plausibly as a subversion of authority for humorous purposes than as a survival of folk magic.[3] Historian Brian Levack,* on the other hand, supports Thomas's thesis that the main cause of

> ❝ Thirty-eight years after its publication, *Religion and the Decline of Magic* remains a central influence on our understanding of Renaissance* culture.[1] ❞
>
> Theodore K. Rabb,* "Review of Keith Thomas, *Religion and the Decline of Magic*," *The Sixteenth Century Journal*

witchcraft* accusations in early modern England was social tension in small communities.[4]

The topics and methods found in *Religion* are also a fertile ground for broader discussion.

One area in which Religion has prompted discussion is the continuing debate over the view that the Protestant Reformation signaled a triumph of rationality over superstition, on the one hand, and the origins of modernity, on the other. This is an idea associated with the celebrated German sociologist Max Weber,* and his theory of "disenchantment with the world" (*Entzauberung der Welt*).[5] One recent reassessment of this debate associates Thomas's work with this Weberian thesis, while still acknowledging the cautious way in which Thomas outlines his view of the decline of magic: "Despite the studiously agnostic, anthropological spirit in which he conducted his enquiry, [Thomas] too subscribed implicitly to the view that the Reformation helped to emancipate the English populace from a 'superstitious' understanding of the world around them, from assumptions which … were now rightly disdained by intelligent persons."[6]

Here, Thomas's argument is interpreted (perhaps unfairly) as setting magic and reason in opposition to one another—a stance that is now, in many quarters, considered to be anachronistic, and itself an echo of "the rhetoric of rationality and enlightenment" that was part of the way early Protestantism attempted to represent itself.[7]

Interaction

Religion still provokes comment and debate about the usefulness of interdisciplinary* studies—more specifically, whether the methods of history and anthropology can be successfully combined. Despite frequently illustrating points in *Religion* by using the discipline of anthropology, Thomas himself said people should be cautious about using the interdisciplinary method. In the mid-1970s he clearly described the problems historians faced making cross-cultural comparisons.[8]

Both historians and anthropologists continued to debate the relative merits of interdisciplinary studies over the following decades. Some emphasized the subjects and goals shared by the two disciplines, while arguing that the potential for collaboration was limited. No one had succeeded in developing a conceptual framework to account for social change that historians and anthropologists might share.[9]

In 1990, anthropologist Clifford Geertz* commented on contemporary views of the interaction between history and anthropology.[10] Although others saw the disciplines as being in conflict, and considered interdisciplinary studies as undermining the academic rigor of both fields, Geertz saw these fears as unfounded. He believed that the association of history and anthropology was "no mere fashion" and that it would "survive the enthusiasms it generates, the fears it induces and the confusions it causes," even if what it would lead to "in surviving, is distinctly less clear."[11]

Despite this view, skepticism about the mutual benefits of an interaction between history and anthropology has been seen in more recent scholarship.

One assessment emphasizes the fundamental differences between the two disciplines, arguing that if social and cultural histories are to gain from the application of anthropological methods, then assumptions about anthropological analysis must be rethought to be appropriate to the times. As Professor Gerald Sider* wrote: "Much has been written about history and anthropology; indeed, the topic became a fad that is now fortunately coming to an end … the potential of this conjunction may still be significant, but the interweaving of the two disciplines … probably needs to be rebuilt from scratch."[12]

The Continuing Debate

In the years since publication *Religion* has prompted debate about Thomas's key argument that the sixteenth and seventeenth centuries saw an overall decline in the magical way of thinking.

Conducted by specialists working on in-depth studies of a particular area, and incorporating sources that Thomas may have overlooked, these discussions should nonetheless be seen as refinements rather than criticisms of Thomas's thesis.

Scholars of astrology,* for example, have questioned whether the early modern belief in astrology really declined as Thomas suggested, arguing that much of his evidence on the subject is "anecdotal" (that is, based more on individual accounts than scientific evaluation), and a more complete survey of the sources is needed.[13] Others, working in the field of witchcraft studies, see Thomas as making a distinction between "magic" and "science" that is no longer plausible for this period. They have argued that his account failed to draw on a systematic analysis of the available archival material.[14]

NOTES

1   Theodore K. Rabb, "Review of Keith Thomas, *Religion and the Decline of Magic*," *The Sixteenth Century Journal* 40, no. 1 (2009): 132.

2   See Academy of Arts and Sciences, "Hundred Most Influential Books Since the War," *Bulletin of the American Academy of Arts and Sciences* 49 (1996): 12–18.

3   David Cressy, *Travesties and Transgressions in Tudor and Stuart England: Tales of Discord and Dissension* (Oxford, Oxford University Press; 2000), 183–4.

4   Brian Levack, *The Witch-Hunt in Early Modern Europe*, 3rd ed. (London: Routledge, 2006), 136.

5   Translated as "elimination of magic from the world" in Max Weber, *The Protestant Ethic and the Spirit of Capitalism* (London: Allen and Unwin, 1930), 105.

6   Alexandra Walsham, "The Reformation and 'The Disenchantment of the World' Reassessed," *The Historical Journal* 51 (2008): 499.

7   Walsham, "The Reformation and 'The Disenchantment of the World' Reassessed": 505.

8   Keith Thomas, "An Anthropology of Religion and Magic, II," *Journal of Interdisciplinary History* 6 (1975), 107.

9   Bernard S. Cohn, "History and Anthropology: the State of Play," *Comparative Studies in Society and History* 22, no. 2 (1980): 198–9.

10 Clifford Geertz, "History and Anthropology," *New Literary History* 21, no. 2 (1990): 321–35.

11 Geertz, "History and Anthropology," 333.

12 Gerald Sider, "Anthropology and History: Opening Points for a New Synthesis," in *Critical Junctions: Anthropology and History beyond the Cultural Turn*, ed. Don Kalb and Herman Tak (Oxford: Berghahn Books, 2005), 168.

13 See, for example, Lauren Kassell, *Medicine and Magic in Elizabethan London: Simon Forman, Astrologer, Alchemist, and Physician* (Oxford: Oxford University Press, 2005), 127–30.

14 Jonathan Barry, *Witchcraft and Demonology in South-West England, 1640–1789* (London: Palgrave Macmillan, 2012), 4–5; Malcolm Gaskill, "Witchcraft in Early Modern Kent: Stereotypes and the Background to Accusations," in *Witchcraft in Early Modern Europe: Studies in Culture and Belief*, ed. Jonathan Barry et al. (Cambridge: Cambridge University Press, 1996), 284–5; Emma Wilby, *Cunning Folk and Familiar Spirits: Shamanistic Visionary Traditions in Early Modern British Witchcraft and Magic* (Eastbourne: Sussex Academic Press, 2005), 51.

MODULE 12
WHERE NEXT?

KEY POINTS

- Despite challenges to its central thesis, *Religion* remains a core text in its field. Thomas is one of the most respected English historians and continues to be active in debate.

- In recent years the field of magic* studies has progressed into areas Thomas did not consider in detail: necromancy* and monsters, for example.

- *Religion* is a key work, having influenced subsequent research in the histories of magic, religion, and science. It represents a watershed moment in the development of historical anthropology.

Potential

Although not everyone today accepts its central argument, Keith Thomas's *Religion and the Decline of Magic* remains, by consensus, a very important text, offering the richest account of popular beliefs in sixteenth- and seventeenth-century England.

In it, Thomas highlights how distinct areas of belief—even as apparently disparate as witches,* omens, prophecies,* and fairies—could be considered together to map changes in the thought of a historical period. It seems likely *Religion* will continue to be required reading for people interested in the history of popular belief in early modern* England and those who believe history can be improved through models developed in the social sciences. The fact that *Religion* has recently been republished by in the popular Penguin imprint and also as an e-book shows its lasting popular appeal.

Keith Thomas himself remains a prominent figure in both English academia and cultural public life, although he is less active in research

> **❝** There are many works of history that are revered, but few that are loved as *Religion and the Decline of Magic* is ... It may be that in the light of later research, certain lines of argument in the book can be challenged or amplified. But its richness and freshness are undiminished, and as a source of insight it is unlikely to be superseded.[1] **❞**
>
> Hilary Mantel,* "The Magic of Keith Thomas," *New York Review of Books*

than in the early stages of his career. He recently became involved in a controversy about the nominations for the Wolfson History Prize* (he is chairman of the judging panel) and the effects of the "popularization" of history.[2] Thomas was quoted as saying the growth in popular history has resulted in young academics writing books for an oversubscribed general market rather than producing works of a high scholarly standard.

This prompted responses from commentators about the need for a re-evaluation of how academic success should be judged.[3] Thomas himself later responded to this debate, claiming in the British *Independent** newspaper that his initial comments had been taken out of context and that he believed the state of the discipline to be as healthy as ever.[4] This suggests that, in keeping with the popular tone of *Religion*, Thomas continues to believe that history should be accessible to all.

Future Directions

Religion played a key role in defining the scholarly study of the history of magic and making it credible. And the evidence presented by Thomas on the subjects of witchcraft, popular magical tradition, and astrology* has been used as a starting-point for subsequent research. But recently the field has turned toward topics that are either not covered in Thomas's book, or are not its primary focus.

One example is the topic of ritual* magic and necromancy—the conjuring of spirits to acquire knowledge; Thomas only touches on the subject, because it concerns a learned type of magic carried out by a literate elite rather than the popular forms he was primarily interested in.

Frank Klaassen,* an American academic currently working in this field, agrees with Thomas's view that religion and learned magic were totally intertwined. But he aims to produce a more nuanced account, examining the differences between magical and religious belief in a post-Reformation* context.[5]

Thomas's work also continues to provoke debate in its depiction of medieval Christianity.* A recent compilation of excerpts from key texts discussing medieval Christianity devotes a chapter to *Religion and the Decline of Magic*. The compilation considers Thomas's book to be the perfect example of the view that Christians of the period incorporated many magical beliefs and practices into their religious life.[6] The editor of this volume positions Thomas at the center of the debate about the extent to which Western society was defined by traditional Christian belief during the Middle Ages.* The editor also encourages the reader to consider the implications of Thomas's work for current scholarship in the field.

Summary

As is inevitable with any work, some of *Religion*'s approaches and conclusions have dated in the decades since it was written. As Thomas himself recently stated: "Any history book will tell its reader as much about the period in which it was written as about the period it seeks to describe. It cannot help being a cultural product, shot through with the values and mental assumptions of its time."[7] Despite this, *Religion* retains both its relevance for the study of early modern popular belief and its reputation as a seminal work of cultural history.

There are a number of reasons for this. The first stems from the book's broad social historical* perspective, which draws on areas of inquiry previously considered inappropriate for academic study. *Religion* has proved influential in establishing new fields of research in the area of cultural history.

The second concerns the wealth of primary source material Thomas examined. This remains unsurpassed in scope and is considered an important resource for current research.

The third relates to Thomas's historical method, which draws on approaches associated with anthropology and other social sciences. While the merits of this approach have been debated, Thomas's innovative application of social theory to historical source material is still influential today.

NOTES

1 Hilary Mantel, "The Magic of Keith Thomas," *The New York Review of Books*, June 7, 2012, accessed February 13, 2015, http://www.nybooks.com/articles/archives/2012/jun/07/magic-keith-thomas/.

2 Cahal Milmo, "Young Historians 'Are Damaging Academia' in their Bid for Stardom," The *Independent*, May 9, 2012, accessed February 14, 2015, http://www.independent.co.uk/life-style/history/young-historians-are-damaging-academia-in-their-bid-for-stardom-7723284.html.

3 Antony Beevor, "A Limited Idea of Academic Success is the Problem," The *Independent*, May 9, 2012, accessed February 14, 2015, http://www.independent.co.uk/voices/commentators/antony-beevor-a-limited-idea-of-academic-success-is-the-problem-7723285.html.

4 Keith Thomas, Letters: "History Marches On," The *Independent*, May 30, 2012, accessed February 23, 2015, http://www.independent.co.uk/voices/letters/letters-all-equal-subjects-of-a-monarch-7800885.html.

5 Frank Klaassen, *The Transformations of Magic: Illicit Learned Magic in the Later Middle Ages and Renaissance* (University Park, Pennsylvania: Pennsylvania State University Press, 2012).

6 James L. Halverson, ed., *Contesting Christendom: Readings in Medieval Religion and Culture* (Lanham: Rowman and Littlefield, 2008), 207–18.

7 Keith Thomas, "Review of John Burrow, *A History of Histories*," *Guardian*, December 15, 2007, accessed February 14, 2015, http://www.theguardian.com/books/2007/dec/15/featuresreviews.guardianreview6.

GLOSSARY

GLOSSARY OF TERMS

Annales school: one of the dominant twentieth-century schools of history study. Coming out of France, and founded by Marc Bloch* and Lucien Febvre,* the school was in favor of examining many different factors to understand the past, such as social history* and historical mentalities* (that is, the world views of the past).

Astrology: a system of prediction or divination* based on the belief that astronomical phenomena influence the human world. Using astrological charts and horoscopes, its practitioners claim to be able to predict future events, and explain aspects of human character.

British Empire: the collective term for those territories ruled by Britain between the late sixteenth and twentieth centuries. During the nineteenth and early twentieth centuries, it was the predominant global power, comprising a quarter of the world's landmass.

The British Humanist Association: an organization founded in 1896 that attempts to promote a system of ethics independent from religious beliefs ("secular humanism").

Cabala (also spelt Kabbalah): a set of philosophical teachings originating in Judaism. During the medieval and early modern* periods it was the basis for many learned magical* practices.

Celestial bodies: a general term referring to any astronomical object observable in the universe. This includes stars, planets, moons, and asteroids.

Christianity: one of the major world religions along with Islam, Hinduism, Buddhism, and Judaism. It is based on the life and teachings of Jesus Christ, recorded in the New Testament of the Bible. The Christian Church comprises a number of different denominations, the three largest of which are the Protestant,* Roman Catholic,* and Eastern Orthodox churches.

Communist Party Historians Group: a group of English Marxist* historians, founded in 1946. It included some of the most influential historians of postwar Britain, including Christopher Hill,* E. P. Thompson,* Eric Hobsbawm,* and Raphael Samuel.

Consecrated: consecration is the dedication of a person, item, or place to a religious purpose, after which they have a religious or spiritual significance.

Contemporary Sociology: an academic journal of sociology and related disciplines, founded in 1972 and published by SAGE publications in association with the American Sociological Association.

Cultural turn: a movement in the social sciences and humanities that arose in the 1970s and peaked in the 1980s. Cultural turn enthusiasts believed the study of culture to find historical meaning in language and "cultural production."

Demystification: literally, the process of clarification, or the removal of mystery and confusion. In this context, it refers to the decline in superstitious and mystical* beliefs in the West in the aftermath of the scientific advances of the Enlightenment* period of the late seventeenth century.

Divination: a means of reading the hidden meaning of events or foreseeing the future through practices such as astrology,* crystal-gazing, and throwing dice or bones; originally understood as a way of discovering the will of the gods.

Early modern period: the historical period following the Middle Ages* and preceding the modern era. The exact dates of this period are a matter for debate, but are generally accepted to be in the range 1500–1800.

English Civil War: a war fought between King and Parliament between 1642 and 1651. It led to great political and social instability in England.

Empirical: empiricism is the belief that knowledge can only be acquired via the senses; in other words, through observation and testing of hypotheses. It is commonly viewed as the basis for the scientific method.

English Reformation: a period in English history that began in 1529 with King Henry VIII's annulment of his marriage to Catherine of Aragon. It led to England's break with the Roman Catholic Church and the creation of Anglicanism, an English version of Protestantism.

Enlightenment: a Europe-wide intellectual movement that arose in the late seventeenth century. It put reason, rather than superstition or religion, at the heart of all human endeavors.

Eschatology: a branch of theology concerned with the end of human existence. On an individual level, this includes the idea of the "afterlife," the experience of the human soul after the death of its physical form.

Ethnography: a branch of the social sciences that examines people and cultures. It may also be used as a noun, to describe a detailed study of a particular social or cultural group.

Fatalistic: fatalism is a world view that sees all human endeavor as subject to fate (an independent, predetermined course of events).

Functionalism: a theory in the social sciences that views society as a system of interdependent structures designed to promote stability. In this view, all aspects of a society are interpreted as having a definite function or role in the survival of that society.

Holy water: water that has been blessed by a figure of religious authority. In Christianity,* holy water is a key component in rituals such as baptism.

The *Independent*: a British national newspaper, launched in 1986. It is not affiliated with any political party, and features articles presenting a range of both left- and right-wing political views.

Intellectual history: the study of the history of thinkers, of traditions of thought, and of ideas—and of how ideas have been expressed and are related to one another.

***Journal of Interdisciplinary History*:** an academic journal published by MIT Press. It publishes essays and articles that aim to link history with other academic disciplines, such as economics and demography (the study of human populations).

Labour: the Labour Party of Great Britain is a center-left political party. Along with the Conservatives, it is one of the two main political parties of the country. It developed out of the socialist and trade union movements of the late nineteenth century.

Magic: a general term referring to the belief in supernatural forces, and the attempt to influence the physical world by means of these forces. It has different connotations in different cultures and at different times.

Marxism: a school of social and economic thought derived from the ideas of Karl Marx and Friedrich Engels that influenced the development of the socialist and Communist movements. Its key ideas are based around class struggle, the overthrow of the bourgeoisie by the proletariat and the replacement of a capitalist system with socialism.

History of mentalities: a historical approach associated with the Annales* movement. The term, taken from the French *histoire des mentalités*, describes the study of attitudes, beliefs, and world views in past cultures and societies.

Middle Ages: the historical period following the Ancient or Classical era. It is commonly understood to refer to the 1000 years between the fall of the Roman Empire in the West in the fifth century and the beginning of the Renaissance in the fifteenth century.

Mysticism: the belief and practice, common to many religions, of spiritual communion with God or other supernatural beings. This may be attained by such practices as meditation.

Necromancy: a form of magic involving communication with the deceased or with demonic beings for the purposes of obtaining knowledge. It often involves the performance of elaborate rituals.*

Past and Present: an influential British academic journal, founded in 1952 by a group of predominantly Marxist historians. It is published four times a year by the Oxford University Press.

Placebo: a simulated medical treatment designed to deceive the person receiving it. The "placebo effect" describes the way the expectation of being cured can influence recovery from illness.

Prophecy: in this context, the practice of predicting the future, or divining knowledge, via supernatural means. In a specifically religious context, it may also mean communication with and divination of the will of God.

Protestant: Protestantism is a form of Christianity originating with the Protestant Reformation* of the sixteenth century, in which various groups across Europe sought to break away from the Roman Catholic Church. Today, Protestants comprise almost 40 percent of Christians worldwide.

Renaissance: historical period following the Middle Ages, marked by a renewed interest in the arts and learning of Ancient Greece and Rome and a great cultural flowering in Europe. It is traditionally seen as having begun in the fifteenth century.

Ritual magic: a form of magic based on elaborate ceremonial practices. In the premodern period, these rituals were often associated with written instructions or diagrams, and thus confined to the literate elite.

Roman Catholicism: the Roman Catholic Church is the largest and oldest of the Christian denominations. The head of the Catholic Church is the Pope, who resides in the Vatican in Italy. Approximately half of all Christians worldwide are Catholics.

Scientific revolution: a series of advances in mathematics, physics, biology, and chemistry, commonly believed to signal the birth of modern science. These events happened between the sixteenth and the eighteenth centuries.

Scrofula: an old-fashioned term for a disease that led to swelling of the glands. Today, it is believed to have been a form of tuberculosis.

Secularization: the decline in the importance of religious and spiritual belief within a society. It may refer more specifically to the decline in power of religious institutions as a social or political force.

Social anthropology: the study of peoples (anthropology) with a strong emphasis on social and economic relations. This includes such topics as law, family, religion, and gender.

Social history: the study of the past emphasizing the experiences, thought, and relations of everyday individuals.

Solar system: the Sun and the objects that orbit it. The largest of these are the eight planets: Mercury, Venus, Earth, Mars, Jupiter, Saturn, Uranus, and Neptune.

Structuralism: an intellectual movement of the early twentieth century. It is characterized by the belief that human culture and societies are governed by underlying patterns and forces that interact in a larger system.

Theological: theology is the academic study of religion and deities. It is one of the oldest academic disciplines, and shares common ground with the study of philosophy.

Witch: person who practices witchcraft.

Witchcraft: the belief in and practice of magic, for a variety of purposes such as healing or prophecy. The nature of witchcraft and the status of those taking part varies widely according to social and cultural contexts.

Witch-hunts: in this context, witch-hunts refer to the widespread and officially sanctioned persecution of individuals seen to be witches in Europe and North America during the early modern period (c. 1400–c. 1700). More generally, the term can refer to any persecution of a marginalized group.

Wolfson History Prize: a literary award presented annually in the UK for exceptional works in the field of popular history. It was founded in 1972 by the Wolfson Foundation, a charitable trust.

World War II: the global conflict that took place between 1939 and 1945 between Germany, Italy, and Japan (the Axis powers) and Britain, the Soviet Union, the United States, and other nations (the Allies).

PEOPLE MENTIONED IN THE TEXT

Marc Bloch (1886–1944) was a French medieval historian, one of the founding members of the Annales school,* and a pioneer in the fields of comparative history and historical anthropology.

Peter Burke (b. 1937) is a British historian of the cultural history of the Renaissance era and seventeenth-century France. He was long based at the University of Sussex, and is now a Fellow of Emmanuel College, Cambridge.

Euan Cameron is an English expert on the religious history of the medieval and early modern* periods. He is the author of numerous classic studies of the Reformation, and more recently *Enchanted Europe: Superstition, Reason, and Religion, 1250–1750* (2010).

David Cressy (b. 1946) is an American social historian of early modern England. He has published widely on such subjects as literacy, popular and elite religion, migration, and memory.

Johannes Dillinger (b. 1968) is a historian who has studied and taught widely in Britain and Germany. He specializes in the history of magic* and ritual practices in the sixteenth century.

Eamon Duffy (b. 1947) is a Cambridge-based historian famed for his innovative work on the English Reformation.* His best-known work is *The Stripping of the Altars* (1992).

Geoffrey Elton (1921–94) was a German-born British historian of the Tudor period. His most famous works include *The Practice of History* (1967) and *The Tudor Constitution: Documents and Commentary* (1960).

E. E. Evans-Pritchard (1902–73) was a British anthropologist who pioneered social anthropology* in the United Kingdom. His best-known work is *Witchcraft, Oracles, and Magic Among the Azande* (1937).

Lucien Febvre (1878–1956) was an early modern historian and one of the co-founders of the Annales school with Marc Bloch.* He advocated breaking with previous historiographical* traditions in favor of a more holistic view of history.

James Frazer (1854–1941) was a Scottish anthropologist. His seminal text *The Golden Bough: A Study in Magic and Religion*, first published in 1890, pioneered the academic study of myth and ritual.

Clifford Geertz (1926–2006) was an American cultural anthropologist, considered to be one of the most influential of the twentieth century. He was instrumental in formulating the theory of symbolic anthropology.

Hildred Geertz (b. 1929) is an emeritus professor of anthropology at Princeton University. She has carried out fieldwork in Morocco, Java, and Bali and her books include *The Life of a Balinese Temple: Artistry, Imagination, and History in a Peasant Village (2004)*. She was married from 1948 to 1981 to fellow-anthropologist Clifford Geertz.

Christopher Hill (1912–2003) was an English Marxist historian and a specialist in the early modern period based at Oxford University. His main works include *God's Englishman: Oliver Cromwell and the English Revolution* (1970) and *The World Turned Upside Down: Radical Ideas During the English Revolution* (1972).

Eric Hobsbawm (1917–2012) was an English historian of the modern era. His work examined the industrial revolution, capitalism, socialism, and nationalism from a Marxist perspective.

Frank Klaassen is an American scholar of the Middle Ages* and Renaissance focussing on the study of magic, gender, and the history of science. In 2014 he was the recipient of the 2014 Margaret Wade Labarge Prize for his book *The Transformations of Magic*.

Brian P. Levack (b. 1943) is an American historian of early modern Britain and Europe. He has published widely on the topics of witchcraft, law, and nationality.

Alan Macfarlane (b. 1941) is a historian and social anthropologist based in Cambridge. He has conducted research on diverse societies including early modern England, Nepal, and China.

Bronislaw Malinowski (1884–1942) was a Polish anthropologist and ethnographer. His work has been very influential in the study of social systems.

Hilary Mantel (b. 1952) is a British writer of historical fiction. Her works include the Booker-prize winning novels about Tudor England, *Wolf Hall* (2009) and *Bring Up the Bodies* (2012).

Theodore K. Rabb (b. 1937) is a scholar of the cultural and economic history of early modern Europe. He is a professor at Princeton University, and co-founder and editor of the *Journal of Interdisciplinary History*.*

Rossell Hope Robbins (1912–90) was an English literary scholar of the medieval period, based for the majority of his career in the United States. He was the author of *The Encyclopedia of Witchcraft and Demonology* (1959), amongst other works.

Gerald Sider is an American anthropologist of North America. His work examines culture and class in rural communities, with particular emphasis on economic factors.

E. P. Thompson (1924–93) was a British historian, socialist, and political campaigner. He published seminal work on the history of nineteenth-century British radical movements, notably *The Making of the English Working Class* (1963).

Lynn Thorndike (1882–1965) was an American historian who spent most of his academic career at Columbia University. He published widely on medieval and early modern philosophy and science.

Hugh Trevor-Roper (1914–2003) was a British historian, famous for his work on Nazi Germany and early modern England. His best-known work is *The Last Days of Hitler* (1947).

Max Weber (1864–1920) was a German sociologist who connected the end of a magical world view with the rise of Protestantism. Among his many works were *The Protestant Ethic and the Spirit of Capitalism* (1905) and *The City* (1921).

Emma Wilby is a historian of magical belief and witchcraft in early modern Britain. Her most recent book examines the trial for witchcraft of the Scottish woman Isobel Gowdie in 1662.

Frances Yates (1899–1981) was an English historian who studied the history of Western esotericism. In particular, she specialized in the occult philosophical traditions of the Renaissance.

WORKS CITED

WORKS CITED

Academy of Arts and Sciences. "The Hundred Most Influential Books Since the War." *Bulletin of the American Academy of Arts and Sciences* 49 (1996).

Ashton, Robert. "Review of Keith Thomas, *Religion and the Decline of Magic*." *The Economic History Review* 25, no. 2 (May 1972).

Barry, Jonathan. *Witchcraft and Demonology in South-West England, 1640–1789*. London: Palgrave Macmillan, 2012.

Barry, Jonathan, Marianne Hester and Gareth Roberts, eds. *Witchcraft in Early Modern Europe: Studies in Culture and Belief.* Cambridge: Cambridge University Press, 1996.

Beevor, Antony. "A Limited Idea of Academic Success is the Problem." The *Independent*, May 9, 2012. Accessed February 14, 2015. http://www. independent.co.uk/voices/commentators/antony-beevor-a-limited-idea-of-academic-success-is-the-problem-7723285.html.

Briggs, Robin. Witches and Neighbours: The Social and Cultural Context of European Witchcraft. Oxford: Wiley-Blackwell, 2002.

Buccola, Regina. *Fairies, Fractious Women and the Old Faith*. Susquehanna: Susquehanna University Press, 2006.

Burke, Peter. Popular Culture in Early Modern Europe. London: Ashgate, 1978.

What is Cultural History? Cambridge: Cambridge University Press, 2004.

Burke, Peter, Brian Harrison and Paul Slack, eds. *Civil Histories: Essays Presented to Sir Keith Thomas*. Oxford: Oxford University Press, 2000.

Cameron, Euan. *Enchanted Europe: Superstition, Reason, and Religion 1250–1750*. Oxford: Oxford University Press, 2010.

The European Reformation. Oxford: Oxford University Press, 2012.

Calaresu, Melissa. "Introduction: Peter Burke and the History of Cultural History." In *Exploring Cultural History: Essays in Honour of Peter Burke,* edited by Melissa Calaresu, Filippo de Vivo and Joan Pau Rubiés. Farnham: Ashgate, 2010.

Cohn, Bernard S. "History and Anthropology: the State of Play." *Comparative Studies in Society and History* 22: 2 (1980).

Crehan, J. H., ed. *Ghosts and Poltergeists*. Chicago: Henry Regnery Co., 1954.

Cressy, David. *Travesties and Transgressions in Tudor and Stuart England: Tales of Discord and Dissension*. Oxford: Oxford University Press, 2000.

Dillinger, Johannes. *"Evil People": A Comparative Study of Witch Hunts in Swabian Austria and the Electorate of Trier*. Charlottesville: University of Virginia Press, 2009.

Domanska, Ewa. "Interview with Peter Burke." In *Encounters: Philosophy of History After Postmodernism*. Charlottesville: University Press of Virginia, 1998.

Duffy, Eamon. "Common Thoughts", *London Review of Books* 31 (July 2009).

-*The Stripping of the Altars: Traditional Religion in England 1400–1580*. New Haven and London: Yale University Press, 1992.

Geertz, Clifford. "History and Anthropology." *New Literary History* 21: 2 (1990).

Geertz, Hildred. "An Anthropology of Religion and Magic, I." *Journal of Interdisciplinary History* 6 (1975).

Halverson, James L., ed. *Contesting Christendom: Readings in Medieval Religion and Culture*. Lanham: Rowman and Littlefield, 2008.

Hill, Christopher. "Partial Historians and Total History." In *The Collected Essays of Christopher Hill*: *Volume Three, People and Ideas in Seventeenth-Century England*. Amherst: University of Massachusetts Press, 1986.

Hitchcock, James. "Review of Keith Thomas, *Religion and the Decline of Magic*." *The Review of Politics* 34: 3 (1972).

Kassell, Lauren. *Medicine and Magic in Elizabethan London: Simon Forman, Astrologer, Alchemist, and Physician*. Oxford: Oxford University Press, 2005.

Klaassen, Frank. *The Transformations of Magic: Illicit Learned Magic in the Later Middle Ages and Renaissance*. University Park, Pennsylvania: Pennsylvania State University Press, 2012.

Levack, Brian P. *The Witch-Hunt in Early Modern Europe*. 3rd ed. London: Routledge, 2006.

Macfarlane, Alan. "Interview of Sir Keith Thomas—on His Life and Work (September 5, 2009)." Accessed September 14, 2013. http://www.sms.cam.ac.uk/media/1132829.

-"Review of Keith Thomas, *Religion and the Decline of Magic*." *History Today* (1981).

Mantel, Hilary. "The Magic of Keith Thomas." *The New York Review of Books*, June 7, 2012. Accessed February 13, 2015. http://www.nybooks.com/articles/archives/2012/jun/07/magic-keith-thomas/.

Midelfort, H.C. Erik. "Review of *Religion and the Decline of Magic*." *Journal of the American Academy of Religion* 41 (1973).

Milmo, Cahal. "Young Historians 'Are Damaging Academia' in Their Bid for Stardom." *Independent*, May 9, 2012. Accessed February 14, 2015. http://www.independent.co.uk/life-style/history/young-historians-are-damaging-academia-in-their-bid-for-stardom-7723284.html.

Monter, E. William. "Review of Keith Thomas, *Religion and the Decline of Magic*." *Journal of Modern History* 44:2 (1972).

Obeyesekere, Gananath. *The Apotheosis Of Captain Cook: European Mythmaking In The Pacific*. Princeton: Princeton University Press, 1992.

Rabb, Theodore K. "Review of Keith Thomas, *Religion and the Decline of Magic*." *The Sixteenth Century Journal* 40:1, Special Fortieth Anniversary Issue (2009).

Robbins, Rossell Hope. "Review of Keith Thomas, *Religion and the Decline of Magic*." *Renaissance Quarterly* 26: 1 (1973).

Rysman, Alexander. "Review of Keith Thomas, *Religion and the Decline of Magic*." *Contemporary Sociology* 4:2 (1975).

Sahlins, Marshall. *How "Natives" Think: About Captain Cook, for Example*. Chicago: University of Chicago Press, 1995.

Salmon, J. H. M. "History Without Anthropology: A New Witchcraft Synthesis." *Journal of Interdisciplinary History* 19:3 (1989).

Sider, Gerald. "Anthropology and History: Opening Points for a New Synthesis." In *Critical Junctions: Anthropology and History Beyond the Cultural Turn*, edited by Don Kalb and Herman Tak. New York; Oxford: Berghahn Books, 2005.

Spring, David. "Review of Keith Thomas, *Man and the Natural World*." *The American Historical Review* 89: 3 (1984).

Taylor, D. J. "Review of Keith Thomas, *The Ends of Life*." *Independent*, February 13, 2009.

Thomas, Keith. *Age and Authority in Early Modern England*. London: British Academy, 1976.

"An Anthropology of Religion and Magic, II." *Journal of Interdisciplinary History* 6 (1975).

The Ends of Life: Roads to Fulfilment in Early Modern England Oxford: Oxford University Press, 2009.

Man and the Natural World: Changing Attitudes in England, 1500–1800. Oxford: Oxford University Press, 1983.

The Perception of the Past in Early Modern England: The Creighton Trust Lecture 1983. London: University of London, 1983.

"The Relevance of Social Anthropology to the Study of English Witchcraft." In *Witchcraft Confessions and Accusations*, edited by Mary T. Douglas. London, Tavistock Publications, 1970.

Religion and the Decline of Magic: Studies in Popular Beliefs in Sixteenth- and Seventeenth-Century England. London: Penguin, 1991.

"Review of John Burrow, *A History of Histories*." The *Guardian*, December 15, 2007. Accessed February 14, 2015. http://www.theguardian.com/books/2007/dec/15/featuresreviews.guardianreview6.

Rule and Misrule in the Schools of Early Modern England. Reading: University of Reading, 1976.

"The Social Origins of Hobbes' Political Thought." In *Hobbes Studies* edited by Keith Conrad Brown. Oxford: Basil Blackwell, 1965.

"The Tools and the Job." *Times Literary Supplement* (April 7, 1966).

"Ways of Doing Cultural History." In *Balans en perspectief van de Nederlandse cultuurgeschiedenis*, edited by Rik Sanders, Bas Mesters, Reinier Kramer, and Margreet Windhorst. Amsterdam: Rodopi, 1991.

"Women and the Civil War Sects." *Past and Present* 13 (1958).

Thompson, E.P. "Anthropology and the Discipline of Historical Context." *Midland History* 1 (1972).

Thorndike, Lynn. "Review of Witchcraft in Old and New England by George Lyman Kittredge." *Isis* 13:1 (1929).

Trevor-Roper, Hugh. *The European Witch Craze of the Sixteenth and Seventeenth Centuries.* London: Penguin, 1969.

Walsham, Alexandra. "The Reformation and 'The Disenchantment of the World' Reassessed." The Historical Journal 51 (2008).

"Review of *Witchcraft in Early Modern Europe*." *The English Historical Review* 451 (1998).

Waugh, J. Edward. *Church Folklore: A Record of Some Post-Reformation Usages in the English Church, Now Mostly Obsolete.* London: Griffith Farran and Co., 1894.

Weber, Max. *The Protestant Ethic and the Spirit of Capitalism.* London: Allen and Unwin, 1930.

Wilby, Emma. *Cunning Folk and Familiar Spirits: Shamanistic Visionary Traditions in Early Modern British Witchcraft and Magic*. Eastbourne: Sussex Academic Press, 2005.

Wilson, Adrian. "A Critical Portrait of Social History." In *Rethinking Social History: English Society 1570–1920 and its Interpretation*, edited by Adrian Wilson. Manchester: Manchester University Press, 1995.

Yates, Frances. "Review of *Religion and the Decline of Magic*." *The British Journal for the History of Science* 6 (1972).

THE MACAT LIBRARY
BY DISCIPLINE

AFRICANA STUDIES

Chinua Achebe's *An Image of Africa: Racism in Conrad's Heart of Darkness*
W. E. B. Du Bois's *The Souls of Black Folk*
Zora Neale Huston's *Characteristics of Negro Expression*
Martin Luther King Jr's *Why We Can't Wait*
Toni Morrison's *Playing in the Dark: Whiteness in the American Literary Imagination*

ANTHROPOLOGY

Arjun Appadurai's *Modernity at Large: Cultural Dimensions of Globalisation*
Philippe Ariès's *Centuries of Childhood*
Franz Boas's *Race, Language and Culture*
Kim Chan & Renée Mauborgne's *Blue Ocean Strategy*
Jared Diamond's *Guns, Germs & Steel: the Fate of Human Societies*
Jared Diamond's *Collapse: How Societies Choose to Fail or Survive*
E. E. Evans-Pritchard's *Witchcraft, Oracles and Magic Among the Azande*
James Ferguson's *The Anti-Politics Machine*
Clifford Geertz's *The Interpretation of Cultures*
David Graeber's *Debt: the First 5000 Years*
Karen Ho's *Liquidated: An Ethnography of Wall Street*
Geert Hofstede's *Culture's Consequences: Comparing Values, Behaviors, Institutes and Organizations across Nations*
Claude Lévi-Strauss's *Structural Anthropology*
Jay Macleod's *Ain't No Makin' It: Aspirations and Attainment in a Low-Income Neighborhood*
Saba Mahmood's *The Politics of Piety: The Islamic Revival and the Feminist Subject*
Marcel Mauss's *The Gift*

BUSINESS

Jean Lave & Etienne Wenger's *Situated Learning*
Theodore Levitt's *Marketing Myopia*
Burton G. Malkiel's *A Random Walk Down Wall Street*
Douglas McGregor's *The Human Side of Enterprise*
Michael Porter's *Competitive Strategy: Creating and Sustaining Superior Performance*
John Kotter's *Leading Change*
C. K. Prahalad & Gary Hamel's *The Core Competence of the Corporation*

CRIMINOLOGY

Michelle Alexander's *The New Jim Crow: Mass Incarceration in the Age of Colorblindness*
Michael R. Gottfredson & Travis Hirschi's *A General Theory of Crime*
Richard Herrnstein & Charles A. Murray's *The Bell Curve: Intelligence and Class Structure in American Life*
Elizabeth Loftus's *Eyewitness Testimony*
Jay Macleod's *Ain't No Makin' It: Aspirations and Attainment in a Low-Income Neighborhood*
Philip Zimbardo's *The Lucifer Effect*

ECONOMICS

Janet Abu-Lughod's *Before European Hegemony*
Ha-Joon Chang's *Kicking Away the Ladder*
David Brion Davis's *The Problem of Slavery in the Age of Revolution*
Milton Friedman's *The Role of Monetary Policy*
Milton Friedman's *Capitalism and Freedom*
David Graeber's *Debt: the First 5000 Years*
Friedrich Hayek's *The Road to Serfdom*
Karen Ho's *Liquidated: An Ethnography of Wall Street*

The Macat Library By Discipline

John Maynard Keynes's *The General Theory of Employment, Interest and Money*
Charles P. Kindleberger's *Manias, Panics and Crashes*
Robert Lucas's *Why Doesn't Capital Flow from Rich to Poor Countries?*
Burton G. Malkiel's *A Random Walk Down Wall Street*
Thomas Robert Malthus's *An Essay on the Principle of Population*
Karl Marx's *Capital*
Thomas Piketty's *Capital in the Twenty-First Century*
Amartya Sen's *Development as Freedom*
Adam Smith's *The Wealth of Nations*
Nassim Nicholas Taleb's *The Black Swan: The Impact of the Highly Improbable*
Amos Tversky's & Daniel Kahneman's *Judgment under Uncertainty: Heuristics and Biases*
Mahbub Ul Haq's *Reflections on Human Development*
Max Weber's *The Protestant Ethic and the Spirit of Capitalism*

FEMINISM AND GENDER STUDIES

Judith Butler's *Gender Trouble*
Simone De Beauvoir's *The Second Sex*
Michel Foucault's *History of Sexuality*
Betty Friedan's *The Feminine Mystique*
Saba Mahmood's *The Politics of Piety: The Islamic Revival and the Feminist Subject*
Joan Wallach Scott's *Gender and the Politics of History*
Mary Wollstonecraft's *A Vindication of the Rights of Woman*
Virginia Woolf's *A Room of One's Own*

GEOGRAPHY

The Brundtland Report's *Our Common Future*
Rachel Carson's *Silent Spring*
Charles Darwin's *On the Origin of Species*
James Ferguson's *The Anti-Politics Machine*
Jane Jacobs's *The Death and Life of Great American Cities*
James Lovelock's *Gaia: A New Look at Life on Earth*
Amartya Sen's *Development as Freedom*
Mathis Wackernagel & William Rees's *Our Ecological Footprint*

HISTORY

Janet Abu-Lughod's *Before European Hegemony*
Benedict Anderson's *Imagined Communities*
Bernard Bailyn's *The Ideological Origins of the American Revolution*
Hanna Batatu's *The Old Social Classes And The Revolutionary Movements Of Iraq*
Christopher Browning's *Ordinary Men: Reserve Police Batallion 101 and the Final Solution in Poland*
Edmund Burke's *Reflections on the Revolution in France*
William Cronon's *Nature's Metropolis: Chicago And The Great West*
Alfred W. Crosby's *The Columbian Exchange*
Hamid Dabashi's *Iran: A People Interrupted*
David Brion Davis's *The Problem of Slavery in the Age of Revolution*
Nathalie Zemon Davis's *The Return of Martin Guerre*
Jared Diamond's *Guns, Germs & Steel: the Fate of Human Societies*
Frank Dikotter's *Mao's Great Famine*
John W Dower's *War Without Mercy: Race And Power In The Pacific War*
W. E. B. Du Bois's *The Souls of Black Folk*
Richard J. Evans's *In Defence of History*
Lucien Febvre's *The Problem of Unbelief in the 16th Century*
Sheila Fitzpatrick's *Everyday Stalinism*

Eric Foner's *Reconstruction: America's Unfinished Revolution, 1863-1877*
Michel Foucault's *Discipline and Punish*
Michel Foucault's *History of Sexuality*
Francis Fukuyama's *The End of History and the Last Man*
John Lewis Gaddis's *We Now Know: Rethinking Cold War History*
Ernest Gellner's *Nations and Nationalism*
Eugene Genovese's *Roll, Jordan, Roll: The World the Slaves Made*
Carlo Ginzburg's *The Night Battles*
Daniel Goldhagen's *Hitler's Willing Executioners*
Jack Goldstone's *Revolution and Rebellion in the Early Modern World*
Antonio Gramsci's *The Prison Notebooks*
Alexander Hamilton, John Jay & James Madison's *The Federalist Papers*
Christopher Hill's *The World Turned Upside Down*
Carole Hillenbrand's *The Crusades: Islamic Perspectives*
Thomas Hobbes's *Leviathan*
Eric Hobsbawm's *The Age Of Revolution*
John A. Hobson's *Imperialism: A Study*
Albert Hourani's *History of the Arab Peoples*
Samuel P. Huntington's *The Clash of Civilizations and the Remaking of World Order*
C. L. R. James's *The Black Jacobins*
Tony Judt's *Postwar: A History of Europe Since 1945*
Ernst Kantorowicz's *The King's Two Bodies: A Study in Medieval Political Theology*
Paul Kennedy's *The Rise and Fall of the Great Powers*
Ian Kershaw's *The "Hitler Myth": Image and Reality in the Third Reich*
John Maynard Keynes's *The General Theory of Employment, Interest and Money*
Charles P. Kindleberger's *Manias, Panics and Crashes*
Martin Luther King Jr's *Why We Can't Wait*
Henry Kissinger's *World Order: Reflections on the Character of Nations and the Course of History*
Thomas Kuhn's *The Structure of Scientific Revolutions*
Georges Lefebvre's *The Coming of the French Revolution*
John Locke's *Two Treatises of Government*
Niccolò Machiavelli's *The Prince*
Thomas Robert Malthus's *An Essay on the Principle of Population*
Mahmood Mamdani's *Citizen and Subject: Contemporary Africa And The Legacy Of Late Colonialism*
Karl Marx's *Capital*
Stanley Milgram's *Obedience to Authority*
John Stuart Mill's *On Liberty*
Thomas Paine's *Common Sense*
Thomas Paine's *Rights of Man*
Geoffrey Parker's *Global Crisis: War, Climate Change and Catastrophe in the Seventeenth Century*
Jonathan Riley-Smith's *The First Crusade and the Idea of Crusading*
Jean-Jacques Rousseau's *The Social Contract*
Joan Wallach Scott's *Gender and the Politics of History*
Theda Skocpol's *States and Social Revolutions*
Adam Smith's *The Wealth of Nations*
Timothy Snyder's *Bloodlands: Europe Between Hitler and Stalin*
Sun Tzu's *The Art of War*
Keith Thomas's *Religion and the Decline of Magic*
Thucydides's *The History of the Peloponnesian War*
Frederick Jackson Turner's *The Significance of the Frontier in American History*
Odd Arne Westad's *The Global Cold War: Third World Interventions And The Making Of Our Times*

The Macat Library By Discipline

LITERATURE

Chinua Achebe's *An Image of Africa: Racism in Conrad's Heart of Darkness*
Roland Barthes's *Mythologies*
Homi K. Bhabha's *The Location of Culture*
Judith Butler's *Gender Trouble*
Simone De Beauvoir's *The Second Sex*
Ferdinand De Saussure's *Course in General Linguistics*
T. S. Eliot's *The Sacred Wood: Essays on Poetry and Criticism*
Zora Neale Huston's *Characteristics of Negro Expression*
Toni Morrison's *Playing in the Dark: Whiteness in the American Literary Imagination*
Edward Said's *Orientalism*
Gayatri Chakravorty Spivak's *Can the Subaltern Speak?*
Mary Wollstonecraft's *A Vindication of the Rights of Women*
Virginia Woolf's *A Room of One's Own*

PHILOSOPHY

Elizabeth Anscombe's *Modern Moral Philosophy*
Hannah Arendt's *The Human Condition*
Aristotle's *Metaphysics*
Aristotle's *Nicomachean Ethics*
Edmund Gettier's *Is Justified True Belief Knowledge?*
Georg Wilhelm Friedrich Hegel's *Phenomenology of Spirit*
David Hume's *Dialogues Concerning Natural Religion*
David Hume's *The Enquiry for Human Understanding*
Immanuel Kant's *Religion within the Boundaries of Mere Reason*
Immanuel Kant's *Critique of Pure Reason*
Søren Kierkegaard's *The Sickness Unto Death*
Søren Kierkegaard's *Fear and Trembling*
C. S. Lewis's *The Abolition of Man*
Alasdair MacIntyre's *After Virtue*
Marcus Aurelius's *Meditations*
Friedrich Nietzsche's *On the Genealogy of Morality*
Friedrich Nietzsche's *Beyond Good and Evil*
Plato's *Republic*
Plato's *Symposium*
Jean-Jacques Rousseau's *The Social Contract*
Gilbert Ryle's *The Concept of Mind*
Baruch Spinoza's *Ethics*
Sun Tzu's *The Art of War*
Ludwig Wittgenstein's *Philosophical Investigations*

POLITICS

Benedict Anderson's *Imagined Communities*
Aristotle's *Politics*
Bernard Bailyn's *The Ideological Origins of the American Revolution*
Edmund Burke's *Reflections on the Revolution in France*
John C. Calhoun's *A Disquisition on Government*
Ha-Joon Chang's *Kicking Away the Ladder*
Hamid Dabashi's *Iran: A People Interrupted*
Hamid Dabashi's *Theology of Discontent: The Ideological Foundation of the Islamic Revolution in Iran*
Robert Dahl's *Democracy and its Critics*
Robert Dahl's *Who Governs?*
David Brion Davis's *The Problem of Slavery in the Age of Revolution*

Alexis De Tocqueville's *Democracy in America*
James Ferguson's *The Anti-Politics Machine*
Frank Dikotter's *Mao's Great Famine*
Sheila Fitzpatrick's *Everyday Stalinism*
Eric Foner's *Reconstruction: America's Unfinished Revolution, 1863-1877*
Milton Friedman's *Capitalism and Freedom*
Francis Fukuyama's *The End of History and the Last Man*
John Lewis Gaddis's *We Now Know: Rethinking Cold War History*
Ernest Gellner's *Nations and Nationalism*
David Graeber's *Debt: the First 5000 Years*
Antonio Gramsci's *The Prison Notebooks*
Alexander Hamilton, John Jay & James Madison's *The Federalist Papers*
Friedrich Hayek's *The Road to Serfdom*
Christopher Hill's *The World Turned Upside Down*
Thomas Hobbes's *Leviathan*
John A. Hobson's *Imperialism: A Study*
Samuel P. Huntington's *The Clash of Civilizations and the Remaking of World Order*
Tony Judt's *Postwar: A History of Europe Since 1945*
David C. Kang's *China Rising: Peace, Power and Order in East Asia*
Paul Kennedy's *The Rise and Fall of Great Powers*
Robert Keohane's *After Hegemony*
Martin Luther King Jr.'s *Why We Can't Wait*
Henry Kissinger's *World Order: Reflections on the Character of Nations and the Course of History*
John Locke's *Two Treatises of Government*
Niccolò Machiavelli's *The Prince*
Thomas Robert Malthus's *An Essay on the Principle of Population*
Mahmood Mamdani's *Citizen and Subject: Contemporary Africa And The Legacy Of
Late Colonialism*
Karl Marx's *Capital*
John Stuart Mill's *On Liberty*
John Stuart Mill's *Utilitarianism*
Hans Morgenthau's *Politics Among Nations*
Thomas Paine's *Common Sense*
Thomas Paine's *Rights of Man*
Thomas Piketty's *Capital in the Twenty-First Century*
Robert D. Putman's *Bowling Alone*
John Rawls's *Theory of Justice*
Jean-Jacques Rousseau's *The Social Contract*
Theda Skocpol's *States and Social Revolutions*
Adam Smith's *The Wealth of Nations*
Sun Tzu's *The Art of War*
Henry David Thoreau's *Civil Disobedience*
Thucydides's *The History of the Peloponnesian War*
Kenneth Waltz's *Theory of International Politics*
Max Weber's *Politics as a Vocation*
Odd Arne Westad's *The Global Cold War: Third World Interventions And The Making Of Our Times*

POSTCOLONIAL STUDIES

Roland Barthes's *Mythologies*
Frantz Fanon's *Black Skin, White Masks*
Homi K. Bhabha's *The Location of Culture*
Gustavo Gutiérrez's *A Theology of Liberation*
Edward Said's *Orientalism*
Gayatri Chakravorty Spivak's *Can the Subaltern Speak?*

PSYCHOLOGY

Gordon Allport's *The Nature of Prejudice*
Alan Baddeley & Graham Hitch's *Aggression: A Social Learning Analysis*
Albert Bandura's *Aggression: A Social Learning Analysis*
Leon Festinger's *A Theory of Cognitive Dissonance*
Sigmund Freud's *The Interpretation of Dreams*
Betty Friedan's *The Feminine Mystique*
Michael R. Gottfredson & Travis Hirschi's *A General Theory of Crime*
Eric Hoffer's *The True Believer: Thoughts on the Nature of Mass Movements*
William James's *Principles of Psychology*
Elizabeth Loftus's *Eyewitness Testimony*
A. H. Maslow's *A Theory of Human Motivation*
Stanley Milgram's *Obedience to Authority*
Steven Pinker's *The Better Angels of Our Nature*
Oliver Sacks's *The Man Who Mistook His Wife For a Hat*
Richard Thaler & Cass Sunstein's *Nudge: Improving Decisions About Health, Wealth and Happiness*
Amos Tversky's *Judgment under Uncertainty: Heuristics and Biases*
Philip Zimbardo's *The Lucifer Effect*

SCIENCE

Rachel Carson's *Silent Spring*
William Cronon's *Nature's Metropolis: Chicago And The Great West*
Alfred W. Crosby's *The Columbian Exchange*
Charles Darwin's *On the Origin of Species*
Richard Dawkin's *The Selfish Gene*
Thomas Kuhn's *The Structure of Scientific Revolutions*
Geoffrey Parker's *Global Crisis: War, Climate Change and Catastrophe in the Seventeenth Century*
Mathis Wackernagel & William Rees's *Our Ecological Footprint*

SOCIOLOGY

Michelle Alexander's *The New Jim Crow: Mass Incarceration in the Age of Colorblindness*
Gordon Allport's *The Nature of Prejudice*
Albert Bandura's *Aggression: A Social Learning Analysis*
Hanna Batatu's *The Old Social Classes And The Revolutionary Movements Of Iraq*
Ha-Joon Chang's *Kicking Away the Ladder*
W. E. B. Du Bois's *The Souls of Black Folk*
Émile Durkheim's *On Suicide*
Frantz Fanon's *Black Skin, White Masks*
Frantz Fanon's *The Wretched of the Earth*
Eric Foner's *Reconstruction: America's Unfinished Revolution, 1863-1877*
Eugene Genovese's *Roll, Jordan, Roll: The World the Slaves Made*
Jack Goldstone's *Revolution and Rebellion in the Early Modern World*
Antonio Gramsci's *The Prison Notebooks*
Richard Herrnstein & Charles A Murray's *The Bell Curve: Intelligence and Class Structure in American Life*
Eric Hoffer's *The True Believer: Thoughts on the Nature of Mass Movements*
Jane Jacobs's *The Death and Life of Great American Cities*
Robert Lucas's *Why Doesn't Capital Flow from Rich to Poor Countries?*
Jay Macleod's *Ain't No Makin' It: Aspirations and Attainment in a Low Income Neighborhood*
Elaine May's *Homeward Bound: American Families in the Cold War Era*
Douglas McGregor's *The Human Side of Enterprise*
C. Wright Mills's *The Sociological Imagination*

Thomas Piketty's *Capital in the Twenty-First Century*
Robert D. Putman's *Bowling Alone*
David Riesman's *The Lonely Crowd: A Study of the Changing American Character*
Edward Said's *Orientalism*
Joan Wallach Scott's *Gender and the Politics of History*
Theda Skocpol's *States and Social Revolutions*
Max Weber's *The Protestant Ethic and the Spirit of Capitalism*

THEOLOGY

Augustine's *Confessions*
Benedict's *Rule of St Benedict*
Gustavo Gutiérrez's *A Theology of Liberation*
Carole Hillenbrand's *The Crusades: Islamic Perspectives*
David Hume's *Dialogues Concerning Natural Religion*
Immanuel Kant's *Religion within the Boundaries of Mere Reason*
Ernst Kantorowicz's *The King's Two Bodies: A Study in Medieval Political Theology*
Søren Kierkegaard's *The Sickness Unto Death*
C. S. Lewis's *The Abolition of Man*
Saba Mahmood's *The Politics of Piety: The Islamic Revival and the Feminist Subject*
Baruch Spinoza's *Ethics*
Keith Thomas's *Religion and the Decline of Magic*

COMING SOON

Chris Argyris's *The Individual and the Organisation*
Seyla Benhabib's *The Rights of Others*
Walter Benjamin's *The Work Of Art in the Age of Mechanical Reproduction*
John Berger's *Ways of Seeing*
Pierre Bourdieu's *Outline of a Theory of Practice*
Mary Douglas's *Purity and Danger*
Roland Dworkin's *Taking Rights Seriously*
James G. March's *Exploration and Exploitation in Organisational Learning*
Ikujiro Nonaka's *A Dynamic Theory of Organizational Knowledge Creation*
Griselda Pollock's *Vision and Difference*
Amartya Sen's *Inequality Re-Examined*
Susan Sontag's *On Photography*
Yasser Tabbaa's *The Transformation of Islamic Art*
Ludwig von Mises's *Theory of Money and Credit*

Macat Disciplines

Access the greatest ideas and thinkers across entire disciplines, including

INEQUALITY

Ha-Joon Chang's, *Kicking Away the Ladder*

David Graeber's, *Debt: The First 5000 Years*

Robert E. Lucas's, *Why Doesn't Capital Flow from Rich To Poor Countries?*

Thomas Piketty's, *Capital in the Twenty-First Century*

Amartya Sen's, *Inequality Re-Examined*

Mahbub Ul Haq's, *Reflections on Human Development*

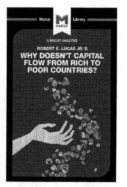

Macat analyses are available from all good bookshops and libraries.

Access hundreds of analyses through one, multimedia tool.

Join free for one month **library.macat.com**

Macat Disciplines

Access the greatest ideas and thinkers across entire disciplines, including

CRIMINOLOGY

Michelle Alexander's
The New Jim Crow: Mass Incarceration in the Age of Colorblindness

Michael R. Gottfredson & Travis Hirschi's
A General Theory of Crime

Elizabeth Loftus's
Eyewitness Testimony

Richard Herrnstein & Charles A. Murray's
The Bell Curve: Intelligence and Class Structure in American Life

Jay Macleod's
Ain't No Makin' It: Aspirations and Attainment in a Low-Income Neighborhood

Philip Zimbardo's
The Lucifer Effect

Macat analyses are available from all good bookshops and libraries.

Access hundreds of analyses through one, multimedia tool.
Join free for one month **library.macat.com**

Macat Disciplines

Access the greatest ideas and thinkers across entire disciplines, including

GLOBALIZATION

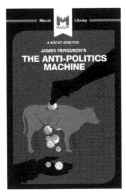

Arjun Appadurai's, *Modernity at Large: Cultural Dimensions of Globalisation*

James Ferguson's, *The Anti-Politics Machine*

Geert Hofstede's, *Culture's Consequences*

Amartya Sen's, *Development as Freedom*

Macat analyses are available from all good bookshops and libraries.

Access hundreds of analyses through one, multimedia tool.
Join free for one month **library.macat.com**

Macat Pairs

Analyse historical and modern issues from opposite sides of an argument. Pairs include:

HOW TO RUN AN ECONOMY

John Maynard Keynes's
The General Theory OF Employment, Interest and Money

Classical economics suggests that market economies are self-correcting in times of recession or depression, and tend toward full employment and output. But English economist John Maynard Keynes disagrees.

In his ground-breaking 1936 study *The General Theory*, Keynes argues that traditional economics has misunderstood the causes of unemployment. Employment is not determined by the price of labor; it is directly linked to demand. Keynes believes market economies are by nature unstable, and so require government intervention. Spurred on by the social catastrophe of the Great Depression of the 1930s, he sets out to revolutionize the way the world thinks

Milton Friedman's
The Role of Monetary Policy

Friedman's 1968 paper changed the course of economic theory. In just 17 pages, he demolished existing theory and outlined an effective alternate monetary policy designed to secure 'high employment, stable prices and rapid growth.'

Friedman demonstrated that monetary policy plays a vital role in broader economic stability and argued that economists got their monetary policy wrong in the 1950s and 1960s by misunderstanding the relationship between inflation and unemployment. Previous generations of economists had believed that governments could permanently decrease unemployment by permitting inflation—and vice versa. Friedman's most original contribution was to show that this supposed trade-off is an illusion that only works in the short term.

Macat analyses are available from all good bookshops and libraries.

Access hundreds of analyses through one, multimedia tool.
Join free for one month **library.macat.com**

Macat Disciplines

Access the greatest ideas and thinkers across entire disciplines, including

THE FUTURE OF DEMOCRACY

Robert A. Dahl's, *Democracy and Its Critics*
Robert A. Dahl's, *Who Governs?*
Alexis De Toqueville's, *Democracy in America*
Niccolò Machiavelli's, *The Prince*
John Stuart Mill's, *On Liberty*
Robert D. Putnam's, *Bowling Alone*
Jean-Jacques Rousseau's, *The Social Contract*
Henry David Thoreau's, *Civil Disobedience*

Macat analyses are available from all good bookshops and libraries.

Access hundreds of analyses through one, multimedia tool.

Join free for one month **library.macat.com**

Macat Disciplines

Access the greatest ideas and thinkers across entire disciplines, including

TOTALITARIANISM

Sheila Fitzpatrick's, *Everyday Stalinism*
Ian Kershaw's, *The "Hitler Myth"*
Timothy Snyder's, *Bloodlands*

Macat analyses are available from all good bookshops and libraries.

Access hundreds of analyses through one, multimedia tool.

Macat Pairs

Analyse historical and modern issues from opposite sides of an argument. Pairs include:

RACE AND IDENTITY

Zora Neale Hurston's
Characteristics of Negro Expression

Using material collected on anthropological expeditions to the South, Zora Neale Hurston explains how expression in African American culture in the early twentieth century departs from the art of white America. At the time, African American art was often criticized for copying white culture. For Hurston, this criticism misunderstood how art works. European tradition views art as something fixed. But Hurston describes a creative process that is alive, ever-changing, and largely improvisational. She maintains that African American art works through a process called 'mimicry'—where an imitated object or verbal pattern, for example, is reshaped and altered until it becomes something new, novel—and worthy of attention.

Frantz Fanon's
Black Skin, White Masks

Black Skin, White Masks offers a radical analysis of the psychological effects of colonization on the colonized.

Fanon witnessed the effects of colonization first hand both in his birthplace, Martinique, and again later in life when he worked as a psychiatrist in another French colony, Algeria. His text is uncompromising in form and argument. He dissects the dehumanizing effects of colonialism, arguing that it destroys the native sense of identity, forcing people to adapt to an alien set of values—including a core belief that they are inferior. This results in deep psychological trauma.

Fanon's work played a pivotal role in the civil rights movements of the 1960s.

Macat analyses are available from all good bookshops and libraries.

Access hundreds of analyses through one, multimedia tool.
Join free for one month **library.macat.com**

Macat Pairs

Analyse historical and modern issues from opposite sides of an argument. Pairs include:

INTERNATIONAL RELATIONS IN THE 21ST CENTURY

Samuel P. Huntington's
The Clash of Civilisations

In his highly influential 1996 book, Huntington offers a vision of a post-Cold War world in which conflict takes place not between competing ideologies but between cultures. The worst clash, he argues, will be between the Islamic world and the West: the West's arrogance and belief that its culture is a "gift" to the world will come into conflict with Islam's obstinacy and concern that its culture is under attack from a morally decadent "other."

Clash inspired much debate between different political schools of thought. But its greatest impact came in helping define American foreign policy in the wake of the 2001 terrorist attacks in New York and Washington.

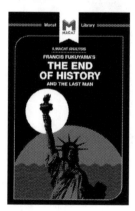

Francis Fukuyama's
The End of History and the Last Man

Published in 1992, *The End of History and the Last Man* argues that capitalist democracy is the final destination for all societies. Fukuyama believed democracy triumphed during the Cold War because it lacks the "fundamental contradictions" inherent in communism and satisfies our yearning for freedom and equality. Democracy therefore marks the endpoint in the evolution of ideology, and so the "end of history." There will still be "events," but no fundamental change in ideology.

Macat Disciplines

Access the greatest ideas and thinkers across entire disciplines, including

MAN AND THE ENVIRONMENT

The Brundtland Report's, *Our Common Future*
Rachel Carson's, *Silent Spring*
James Lovelock's, *Gaia: A New Look at Life on Earth*
Mathis Wackernagel & William Rees's, *Our Ecological Footprint*

Macat analyses are available from all good bookshops and libraries.

Access hundreds of analyses through one, multimedia tool.
Join free for one month **library.macat.com**

Macat Pairs

Analyse historical and modern issues from opposite sides of an argument. Pairs include:

Macat Pairs

Analyse historical and modern issues from opposite sides of an argument. Pairs include:

HOW WE RELATE TO EACH OTHER AND SOCIETY

Jean-Jacques Rousseau's
The Social Contract

Rousseau's famous work sets out the radical concept of the 'social contract': a give-and-take relationship between individual freedom and social order.

If people are free to do as they like, governed only by their own sense of justice, they are also vulnerable to chaos and violence. To avoid this, Rousseau proposes, they should agree to give up some freedom to benefit from the protection of social and political organization. But this deal is only just if societies are led by the collective needs and desires of the people, and able to control the private interests of individuals. For Rousseau, the only legitimate form of government is rule by the people.

Robert D. Putnam's
Bowling Alone

In *Bowling Alone*, Robert Putnam argues that Americans have become disconnected from one another and from the institutions of their common life, and investigates the consequences of this change.

Looking at a range of indicators, from membership in formal organizations to the number of invitations being extended to informal dinner parties, Putnam demonstrates that Americans are interacting less and creating less "social capital" – with potentially disastrous implications for their society.

It would be difficult to overstate the impact of *Bowling Alone*, one of the most frequently cited social science publications of the last half-century.

Macat analyses are available from all good bookshops and libraries.

Access hundreds of analyses through one, multimedia tool.

Join free for one month **library.macat.com**

Printed in the United States
by Baker & Taylor Publisher Services